JEFF FENECH
I love youse all

First published 1993 by Modern Publishing Group
Edited by Andrew Ballard
Typesetting Printworks Publishing
Made and printed in Australia by
McPherson's Printing Group

Trade distribution
Penguin Books Australia Ltd
487 Maroondah Hwy, PO Box 257,
Ringwood, Victoria, Australia, 3134.

All rights reserved.
Other than permitted by Copyright law no part of this publication can be reproduced, copied or transmitted in any form or means electronic, mechanical, photocopying, recording, storage in a retrieval system or otherwise, without prior consent of the publisher.

PROUDLY AUSTRALIAN
THIS BOOK IS 100% AUSTRALIAN PRODUCED,
USING EXCLUSIVELY AUSTRALIAN PAPER,
LABOR AND MATERIALS.

ISBN 1 875 481 370

JEFF FENECH

About Terry Smith

Terry Smith has spent a lifetime attending sporting events in all parts of the world. He has covered championship fights in America and London, Wallaby rugby tours of the British Isles, France and South Africa, the Open golf championships of the United States and Britain, cricket at Lord's and sumo wrestling in Japan. Now boxing and rugby writer for the Sydney Telegraph Mirror, he has written eleven books. He lives in Sydney with wife Sybilla, sons Justin and Roger and a whippet called Bones.

Publisher's acknowledgments

Back cover photograph by Guy Willmott.

Ginger Meggs cartoon by James Kemsley.

We'd like to thank the publishers and editors of the various newspapers and magazines for the photographs, press clippings and cartoons published in this edition, and for their contribution to the life story of Jeff Fenech.

Jeff Fenech at the age of two.

JEFF FENECH

Contents

Introduction — *Alan Jones*   *page 1*

Foreword — *James Packer*   *page 3*

Preface One
Mary Fenech   *page 5*

Preface Two
Johnny Lewis   *page 12*

Chapter One
*The World and My Whole
Life In Front of Me*   *page 19*

Chapter Two
Street Kid   *page 27*

Chapter Three
Olympic Robbery   *page 40*

Chapter Four
World Champion in 196 Days   *page 49*

Chapter Five
World Title II   *page 63*

Chapter Six
World Title III   *page 75*

Chapter Seven
Punch-up in Atlantic City   *page 96*

Chapter Eight
Comeback — page 104

Chapter Nine
Cheated in Las Vegas — page 113

Chapter Ten
Azumah II — page 130

Chapter Eleven
Mates and Ex-mates — page 143

Chapter Twelve
Break-even Bill — page 159

Chapter Thirteen
The Greengrocer — page 165

Chapter Fourteen
Postscript — page 168

Appendix One
Fitness — page 177

Appendix Two
Career Achievements — page 184

Appendix Three
The Professional Fight Record — page 187

Appendix Four
Letters, press clippings, cartoons — page 191

A special mention

I wear a shirt with the logo Ansett Australia: Choice of Champions. Rob O'Brien and Paul Donovan, of Ansett, are champions, too. Thanks guys, for looking after me throughout my career.

Acknowledgments

I've got so many people to thank for making things easier for me. Paul Lonergan, at the Bryson Hotel in Melbourne, where I seem to have spent more time than anywhere else; Dr Bruce Shepherd for saving my hands with his skilful surgery; Andrew Lazarus, from Andrew's Sporting World at Kingsford, Sydney, and Tony and Terry Randle, from Sport's Bazaar in Melbourne; Elio and Gennaro at the Filicudi restaurant, Fivedock, for the countless hours they've spent cooking my food; Alex and Robert, of The Bamboo Terrace and Bamboo House in Melbourne; Champion Spark Plugs, who remained loyal and supportive even though I lost the fights for which they sponsored me; Sinclair Hyundi, at Penrith; Eugene's leather in Melbourne for dressing me neat and tidy; Harry and George Di Costi, the seafood kings, and Mal and Lisa Fittler, of the Aanuka Beach Resort at Coffs Harbor; Roger Alberti, who in good and bad times supported me, that quality in a person should always be admired; Doug Keffard, for all his professional and sound advice that made sure my future after boxing was secure; Max Markson — there have been plenty of promotional people over the years but with Max you know that when a deal is done everyone is happy, he's one in a million; and Adidas for coming in at the end of my career and being loyal to an Australian. I love youse all!

— *Jeff Fenech.*

Introduction

THE Jeff Fenech autobiography is more than just a story about a young Australian's rise from anonymity to international acclaim; more than a catalogue of extraordinary success in the fiercely unrelenting environment of competitive sport.

It is a story, above all else, of a young man who made it to the top, the background to his rise, the people at the centre of it, much of which, until the publication of this book, remains unknown.

But beyond the historical documentation of where this all began and how it happened, fascinating and almost unbelievable in itself, the Jeff Fenech story is almost a symbol of those things that have characterised Australia's growth and success since its inception as a penal colony; because this is a story of adversity meted out in at least the same proportions as achievement.

It is a story which embodies a timeless message to all young Australians: that with effort, discipline, dedication and the good fortune to have good people around you, you can rise above difficulty and, as the cliche suggests, literally "reach for the stars."

One of the reasons Jeff Fenech became a symbol for millions of Australians was not because of his success, but rather because of the circumstances from which he emerged to secure it.

Those circumstances are documented compellingly in the pages ahead. But time is not always an honest servant. It is easier to remember the world title victories than it is to recall that, at a very young age, Jeff Fenech was, at various times, and sometimes at the same time, the Australian Male Athlete of the Year and Australia's Most Popular Sporting Personality for two successive years; the Variety Club of Australia's Sports Entertainer of the Year and Sports Personality of the Year; the winner of the Caltex/Sun Herald Sportsman of the Year and the World Boxing Council's Boxer of the Decade.

It is a record that looms large in the history of Australian sportsmen and women and sporting achievement. And whatever remains to be done by Jeff Fenech, or by any other Australian sporting achievers in the future, Jeff's sporting record will always occupy a place at the top table.

Of course, there have been downs as well as ups. Just as no human being is without blemish, no sporting achievement is ever untarnished. This story is told warts and all. But it is the coexistence of the almost perfect sportsman alongside the sometimes imperfect human being that makes Jeffrey Fenech identifiably and quintessentially Australian.

Quite simply, the real Jeff Fenech story deserves to be told if for no other reason than the simple truth that the record deserves to be remembered.

— *Alan Jones.*

Foreword

JEFF Fenech is one of the legends of Australian sport. His achievements entitle him to comparison to Bradman, Lindrum, Elliot and the other great names of Australian sporting superstardom.

Jeff has earned his status the only way possible: by consistently competing at the highest level and beating the best the world has to offer. At his peak, he avoided nobody and was comfortably victorious against all world class opponents. Indeed, he was sometimes underrated because he defeated top class opponents so easily that casual observers found it hard to believe that these were fighters from the top drawer of world boxing ranks.

Jeff had dazzling speed, amazing strength for his size, wonderful lightness on his feet and all the attributes that make a great fighter. But, above all, he had courage — not just bravery or even lots of courage like lots of sportsmen, but the sort of fierce determination that refuses to even acknowledge pain, let alone use it as a reason for giving up. At times, his hands were so painful that almost any other fighter in the world would have given up. Not only did Jeff not give up, he fought harder — all the more determined not to let agony beat him.

I believe that this unrelenting determination, allied to his natural skills, was what made him one of those once-in-a-generation sportsmen who is so good that he steals a special place in Australian hearts. In addition, Jeff Fenech was very much a people's champion.

Jeff started life with few of the luxuries that make life easier and he quickly learned what it was like to struggle and battle. When, eventually he conquered life's hardships and became a household name throughout Australia, Jeff's head was exactly the same size as it had been when nobody knew who he was. He demonstrated that he was one of those rare people who could make it to the top of the mountain but not look down on anybody.

— *James Packer.*

Preface One

Mary Fenech

WHEN Mary Fenech went to Crown Street Hospital to have her sixth child in May, 1964, she spent four days in labour with what she thought must have been twins.

"My God," she thought, "I have five kids living in two bedrooms and I'm going to take another two home." She rang her husband and cried.

In the end it was just Jeffrey Fenech who went home to the little cottage in Fig Street, Pyrmont, where his dad Paul had not long before become an invalid pensioner — he had suffered a near fatal heart attack.

Little could Mary have dreamed that her fourth son would become a world champion who aroused such passions that idiots would hurl eggs against her door in the middle of the night. She would have to change her silent phone number half a dozen times because of threatening calls. Yet just a few suburbs away that same son was getting good luck calls from Prime Minister Bob Hawke.

The street in St Peters, where Mary Fenech has lived ever since just after Jeff was born, leads down to a park badly in need of a trim. Working class battlers live here. People who call a spade a spade.

A tiny, kindly woman whose brown eyes sparkle behind big glasses, she likes to sit in the spic and span lounge room of her white weatherboard home. The house is adorned with pictures of her children, grandchildren and a large tapestry of the Last Supper. Life was never easy for little Mary Aquilina, as she was before marrying in Australia. She was brought up in Malta during the war years:

'My mother had thirteen kids, and I had to stay home to help her look after the younger ones. I can't read or write because they wouldn't let me go to school. With the Germans bombing us, it was hard during the war in my country. Seven of my brothers and sisters were killed, but my mother had twins when the war finished in 1944.

Although my father had a job as a truck driver in the army after the war, he decided to come to Australia to give us a better life. With my four sisters and brother, we lived in a small place in Elizabeth Street near Redfern Oval. I wasn't allowed to go out anywhere, just follow in my father's and mother's footsteps, so I used to walk home from my job making handbags in the city. That was my outing. Walking home instead of catching the bus. That's how I met my husband Paul. His brother used to come swimming where I used to live in Malta, and they came up and started talking to us.

Paul was a good-looking fellow, very handsome. When we married, I was just sixteen years old. We lived

I LOVE YOUSE ALL

in a one-room place in Crown Street, but by the time we had five kids, it was just too small. We moved into a two-bedroom house in Pyrmont just before you get to the bridge. Two bedrooms upstairs and another room and little kitchen downstairs. With Jeff arriving, we needed a house with a nice backyard, so we looked and looked and found a place in St Peters.

Paul was a healthy man until he had that heart attack one night when he went upstairs to check if the kids were covered. He called down, "They're alright." Then he collapsed at the top of the stairs and for an instant he was dead. He fell down the stairs, bump, bump, bump. The bumping brought him back to life, but he nearly had a broken neck and he had concussion for nearly nine months. And he was only 32 years old. '

Jeff Fenech adores his mother. He has renovated her house, bought her a car and pays all the bills. Once for Mother's Day he presented her with a mink coat in the ring after one of his world title fights. Fearing the worst, he told her not to be at ringside when he had his last fight with Calvin Grove.

' Jeffrey was never really a bad boy because he has a good heart, but he always had a temper. It's in the blood. He can't help it and I'm sure that is what made him a champion. That and his guts. You can't let people come and hit you and tell you off and just stand still. Jeff would never take that and I wouldn't myself. I've been in clubs playing the pokies and people would pick on me and say "What a rotten son you've got." That really hurts, but I tell them off. I know how to answer them. I'm real lucky I've got Jeff because he helps me a lot. All of us, he helps. I always worry about him even now because he opens his heart to everything, good or bad.

I know Jeffrey won three world titles, but I always felt he could have done better if he had better breathing. When he was young, he had an operation on his nose after someone hit him with a bat. It wasn't a success, but he wouldn't stay in hospital so the doctors could do it again. Jeffrey just jumped out of bed and said, "Tomorrow I'm playing football."

With the asthma, too, he always had breathing problems after that. I don't know where that asthma comes from because nobody else in our family has had it. My mother is 87, and she's healthy and everything. I worry about Jeffrey in that Melbourne weather which can change four times a day. It's no good for him. **'**

With her husband on an invalid pension, Mary would take toddler Jeff with her when she worked nights as a cleaner to boost the family income. She'd be quickly home to get the kids off to the school and then she'd visit her husband in hospital. Often little Jeff would be left in the care of the local nuns. As she did with her other five children, Mary would make little suits and dress him up. As a boy, Fenech was rugby league nutty, even making mother train and play with him, as she recalls:

' Jeffrey used to make me run with him in the afternoon down at the park. To please him, I had to. They used to make me play, too. All the mothers got involved,

I LOVE YOUSE ALL

and I was the littlest one. The others were giants.

When he was thirteen or fourteen, I hoped Jeff might get a job in the bank, but none of my sons like dressing with a coat and tie. Instead, he became an apprentice bricklayer, where they used to pick on him a lot. They'd pinch his thermos and tools and break down the walls after he'd put them up.

Jeff was always crazy about sports, but when he took up boxing I was horrified. My God, he'll have to defend himself on his own, I thought. In football he had another twelve guys out there to help. I told him "Don't you go and play boxing."

At first my husband didn't want me to go to the fights. I went to a couple of the little clubs when Jeff started fighting and he kept winning and after a while I got really excited because I was sure he was going to make it. I was sure he'd win the world title, and when he beat Satoshi Shingaki all the family was so happy and proud. Every one of us went to the Marrickville Hotel for the big party. Jerome Coffee was a terrific fight, but my favourite was when Jeff beat the English bloke, John Farrell, in Brisbane. Paul and I went up by train, but the trip was too hot and too long. After that Jeff started paying for us to go everywhere by plane. **'**

There have been plenty of heartaches for Mary Fenech, too: the Los Angeles Olympics, Las Vegas where Jeff was cheated out of his fourth world title by the judges who gave Azumah Nelson a draw; the knockout at Nelson's hands in Melbourne; and then the last hurrah against Calvin Grove. On each occasion she shed a mother's tears:

❝ I cried for Jeff when he lost at the Olympic Games. All of us were broken-hearted for him, especially my husband, who was very cranky. We'd done so much to save up a bit of money to get him to the Games even though we had nothing.

It was the same when he fought Azumah Nelson in Las Vegas. I cried because he really won that fight. I tried to get down to the ring to comfort him, but they had so many security people I couldn't get through.

I was terrified when Azumah knocked him down in the first round of their return fight in Melbourne. He was just lost and blinking, and didn't know where he was.

When I'd gone to his hotel room to iron his dressing gown and trunks like I always did before his fights, Jeff wasn't himself. He was in the bathroom, putting some drops in his ears, which seemed funny, and he made me stay in the hotel until the last minute before going to the ground. I was sure Jeffrey was going to win because of the way he beat Azumah Nelson in Las Vegas, but something happened to him that afternoon. He must have been weakened by all the tablets and stuff they gave him for his flu and asthma. ❞

Mary Fenech's left hand was heavily bandaged following surgery to remove some cysts.:

❝ I had an operation on my hands two months ago and it was brutal. I still can't make a fist. I can't do nothing. What guts Jeff had to have to stand in the ring with those hands for all those fights. I look at his hands and my heart aches for him. I cry sometimes. My husband Paul was a good, hard man, but I think Jeff's guts come from my father's family. They were all fighters.

I've watched and watched the tapes of the Calvin Grove fight, and I'm sure Jeff would have won it if he had put his mind to it. His hands were way down low when Grove knocked him out. I remember when he was hit in one of his earlier fights, and I asked, "Why didn't you cover, Jeff?" He said his hands were so painful that he'd rather be hit on the face than the hands. That's crazy. Why keep fighting if you can't hold your hands up to defend yourself?

My heart is telling me that he might go back, and I just hope God listens when I ask that he stops where he is. It would break my heart. How could he stand in the ring with those hands? It frightens me. **'**

Mary Fenech is delighted by what her son has achieved, but she's adamant that as a fighter he was never the same after that robbery in Las Vegas:

' That will never go out of Jeffrey. It's the same as the Olympic Games. Deep in his heart he would love that gold medal and the belt he should have got for beating Nelson to be at home with the rest of his trophies. **'**

Preface Two

Johnny Lewis

LEAVE the honking traffic of King Street, Newtown, and walk over the railway bridge. Set back from Angel Street is a pink building marked with graffiti. The Newtown Police Boys' Club is a haven for kids of this battling inner-city suburb. Opposite is the decaying shell of an unused building.

Up the stairs and through the door marked "Boxing Room". The gym is spotless, but with the windows shut the musk of sweat hangs in the air. There is the sound of ropes skipping, bags being punched and leathered fists striking raw flesh.

Surveying the scene from one of the corners of the ring is Johnny Lewis, the man who took Jeff Fenech and Jeff Harding to world boxing championships. As competent at his work as a mathematician, as committed to his art as a musician, Lewis has brought dignity and compassion to this most brutal of sports. In world title fights, his boxers have the incredible record of fourteen wins and a draw from sixteen bouts. Even world heavyweight champ Mike Tyson calls him Mr Lewis.

Speaking in his nasally voice, Johnny recalls the day Jeff Fenech first walked through the door of the gym:

❛ Jeff was cheeky, confident and wanted to box straight away. I can never say I visualised world championships and things like that, but I did think, jeez, if this kid can be controlled and disciplined ...

Every day he became keener and keener as if he senses, "Hey, I was born for this. This is what I'm about". I started to hear things about him that didn't surprise me, but through it all stood this terrifically loyal kid. He just had so many things that I liked about him.

To me, if Jeff is your friend, you're a very lucky person. As the years went by, Jeff at times tended to put the real people in his life on hold while he searched for the high rollers, but that is not the real Jeff Fenech. I think he tries too hard to befriend people when there is no need to.

I vividly remember the first time I realised I might have a champion on my hands. I went away once and told him not to fight until I got back. Anyway, he went and had a fight with Tommy Raudonikis in his corner and got beaten by a kid called Joey Glover.

The day I landed at the airport, he was there telling me all about it, how he wanted to fight Glover again, but I was very disappointed that he did what I asked him not to do. I said to Jeff, "Mate, we're going to have four weeks and we're going to beat this bloke." It was just amazing the way Jeff tore this kid to pieces in the return bout. That eye of the tiger that wasn't there when I was looking for it before the fights with Azumah Nelson and Calvin Grove.

Jeff's greatest performance as a professional certainly was the night he beat Victor Callejas to win his third world title. Callejas was a real pocket Mike Tyson, full of dirty backstreet stuff and certainly with a lot of skill. He was ready to take the featherweight division and dominate it for years. There was a little bit of Jeff Fenech in Callejas and a lot of Callejas in Fenech.

Callejas caught Jeff with an absolute boomer in the first round and I'm sure that had he followed up, Jeff would have been in awful trouble. It was a great shot, but the Puerto Rican stood back and admired what he'd done.

In those days the entourage hadn't grown to diabolical proportions, so the disruptions weren't there. Everything was kept in proper perspective. Although the fight with Marcos Villasana was a great performance, I don't think Jeff ever again gave us what he did in stopping Victor Callejas in ten rounds.

I don't think I'll ever meet Jeff's equal as a person. At all times he has been beautiful to myself and my family. Forever and a day, I will say that one of the greatest things in my lifetime has been Jeff Fenech. I got a terrific thrill when he rang up and asked me to be best man at his wedding. I really feel I know him better than anybody else, and I knew he couldn't be beaten unless he beat himself. He allowed cracks to form in the solid foundation, not with me but with the boxing side of it.

I go back a long time with fighters. I used to go down to the old Sydney Stadium and see the cream of Australia's crop dictate and control fights for eight rounds and then succumb to the importations in ten or eleven rounds. We had to get stamina into them. In Jeff Fenech I got the loyal subject who was prepared to work at such a high intensity. In those days Jeff would be first into training and last to leave. He'd go home and have steamed vegetables and live the life you must lead to have success in boxing.

I thought he just beat Azumah Nelson in Las Vegas, but he didn't fight well. Nowhere near his best. We were behind but clawed our way back. Azumah has been a great champion, but he was there for the taking. I don't think he was 50 per cent of his best in Las Vegas. The same in Melbourne.

I didn't want to go to America. I went over there thinking if we didn't knock Azumah out we were going to be dudded, but I honestly don't believe Don King dudded us. That entourage dudded us. Jeff likes to be surrounded by people. but most of them buttered him up and contributed to taking the tiger out of the kid. If the entourage had been cut to an eighth of what was there, we would have had success. Jeff is cunning and certainly street-wise and clever in a lot of things, but he couldn't see they were putting cracks in the foundations that we'd formed. I'm not talking about his promoter Bill Mordey or his friend Peter Mitrevski, the people who really count.

I've got the video of Fenech-Nelson I in my head. There were eight chances we had to jump on Azumah and finish it off, but each time Jeff would allow Azumah back with a flurry. The Jeff Fenech of old would have bombed him out. Azumah was a very proud champion and remained so, and this came through at fight time.

Now it's been documented that Jeff was KOd twice, they say he couldn't take a punch, but I know that he could. He took some really heavy punches. Jeff took a beauty off Samart Payakarun, a tremendous punch off Steve McCrory and a ripper off Victor Callejas. In the first fight with Azumah, he took a few punches that proved still further he was a tough kid.

It wasn't just the women or the doctor that brought him undone in Melbourne before Fenech-Nelson II. I hope I don't get offside with people here, but it was the people in the entourage who should have come down on the day of the fight instead of being there for weeks on end. Their input to the cause was so minimal it was non-existent. Every time Jeff had a headache or a pain in the guts or his bowels were irregular, it was a sign for the doctor to throw him more tablets. I suppose he wanted to justify his existence.

We shouldn't have gone ahead with the Calvin Grove fight. They accused me of not being supportive of it, and I wasn't because Jeff was doing too many wrong things. I've got to be honest. When Jeff was adamant he wanted another shot at Nelson, I grabbed Grove as an opponent because he wasn't a noted puncher. Grove king-hit Jeff because Jeff allowed it to happen. He became frustrated he couldn't throw Calvin around like a rag doll. He thought he could intimidate him, but he couldn't and did his block. Grove just said, "Well, I saw Azumah put one of these on you. I'm going to put one on you, too." And he did.

I think Jeff is too smart a kid ever to get back into a boxing ring. There will certainly be times he'll miss the limelight. Of course, he will. For a while, he virtually had the nation in his hand. I'd like to see him settle down, lead a quiet life for a while and later on get into some high profile stuff as long as it doesn't prompt him into thinking he should resurrect his boxing career. The thought may come into his head, but I believe in Jeff enough to know he'd say "Hey, hang on. I'm not doing this again."

When you think about it, it's almost as if it was an act of God that Jeff and I got together. I was very, very lucky. I could have been away for one or two days when he went to the Newtown Police Boys' Club. He'd have continued to play football and be badly bruised and battered running around as an A Grade footballer, and sent off in a few games here and there. I'd still be working as a signwriter for the Sydney County Council.

I can remember almost every incident in the ten years we've been together. The good times, particularly when there was just Jeff and Peter and I. When Jeff wants to be Jeff, you can have no better friend. There have been a million good times and only a couple of little bad ones. I'm a proud Australian, but I'm also a proud Newtown boy. I suppose I could have moved to a more fashionable address, but Newtown-Erskineville is where I come from and I love the people here. I could move, but I wouldn't be happy anywhere else. ❟

Chapter One

THE WORLD AND MY WHOLE LIFE IN FRONT OF ME

THE buzzer sounds. I stand up and look down at the girl carrying the round card at the Melbourne Tennis Centre. Round seven coming up. Four rounds to go against Calvin Grove and then I'm getting out of boxing forever.

When I win this fight I'm going to hang up the gloves because after two rounds I knew it wasn't there any more. I couldn't pour on the pressure the way I used to. I couldn't work the body and the head and cut off the ring spaces. Nothing was there.

It really hadn't been there since that horror day in Las Vegas when I was robbed of my fourth world boxing title by the judges who made my fight with Azumah Nelson a draw.

When Nelson knocked me out in eight rounds in Melbourne in March, 1992, he didn't fight Jeff Fenech. He fought a zombie. Now I'm back in the ring fifteen months later to wipe the slate clean and let my little boy see me go out a winner. I don't want him to remember Azumah Nelson knocking out his dad. If I won this fight impressively, I was to do my unfinished business with Azumah.

Deep down I knew I was fooling myself. The punches from my sparring partners had started to hurt, and that was a sign that boxing had caught up with me. I'd gone from a boxer who'd sparred light-heavyweights like Jeff Harding and didn't feel a thing to feeling the punches from featherweights in the gym.

I kept trying to make it happen, but I was full of negative thoughts. What if this happens? What if that happens? That was scary because I am such a positive person.

I had had the choice of fighting Grove or Troy Dorsey, but I picked Calvin because he'd just had a narrow loss on points to Nelson at Lake Tahoe, Nevada. When I saw tapes of that bout, I rang my promoter Bill Mordey and thanked him. This would be the easiest fight I've ever had. The American might have a 42-5 record, but he looked very fragile. In the tapes I saw a guy who nearly died of exhaustion against Azumah. Imagine when I put on the pressure.

In the first round, I hit Grove with some hard jabs, some good jabs. He felt them, too. Here is a guy who's supposed to be very, very fast, a great jabber, and I'm taking the jab off him.

It was the same in the second round. I caught him with some good jabs, but I couldn't follow up. My combinations just weren't there. After you jab, things usually fall into place, but I was hitting him with my jab and then couldn't catch him with anything else.

By now the negative thoughts had come crawling in. After the second round, I knew I didn't want to get into a

I LOVE YOUSE ALL

boxing ring ever again. I had nothing left. At the start of each round I'd say to myself: "Seven to go. Six to go." I was counting the rounds to my destiny.

Johnny Lewis, my trainer, kept asking if I was OK. Keep your hands up, he'd say. Keep tidy. He just didn't want me to get hurt. Grove hit me with a few punches, but nothing that really shook me up.

I'll make him fight my fight and get the decision. Hold him, tie him up, work inside, bully him around, just do enough to win. Stay in and get the fight over with. After the third or fourth round I knew I couldn't knock Calvin out. I couldn't hit the guy, not because he's brilliant but because I didn't have anything left. Calvin Grove is a great fighter, but nowhere near the best I've fought. There were many better.

Round seven. I feinted to the right to move from his jab. As I came back, he loaded up for that big right hand that exploded inside my head. Too late I saw it coming. Voom! The lights spun like crazy for a few seconds, then they went out. Jeff Fenech's boxing career was over.

I always preach that boxing is a thinking man's game, but that night I just couldn't think. I got knocked out because my mind wasn't on the job. As much as I would have loved to put my hands up, tuck my chin down and do nothing else, I couldn't do it. It wasn't me. I was frustrated and couldn't do things properly. The guy Calvin Grove fought was a shadow of the real Jeff Fenech.

I don't remember speaking from the ring and heaven knows how long I was in the dressing room before they hustled me out of the centre. It wasn't until then that it really sunk in what had happened. I must have swallowed a lot of blood because the taste of it was in my mouth. Johnny sat with me in the car as I went to the Alfred Hospital for tests.

They asked me a lot of questions. Who was Prime Minister of Australia? What was the date? Who was I? After I'd answered them OK, they x-rayed my jaw and I had brain scans and all that stuff. Then they stitched up my mouth. Twenty-four stitches.

I wasn't drowsy and didn't have any headaches, which was a good sign, and I was in good spirits. At 3am they wanted to keep me in hospital for observation, but I was going back to the hotel where my little boy was waiting. Beau was asleep in my bed, so I climbed in and lay there beside him. I couldn't sleep because the thoughts were racing through my head.

What would people think? I had failed. Jeff Fenech was a loser. If only they knew what I'd gone through to win three world titles for Australia and how I felt. It wasn't Jeff Fenech that Azumah Nelson and now Calvin Grove had knocked out. It wasn't the person I had wanted my supporters to see in the ring.

From the time I had my fourteenth professional fight against Steve McCrory in July, 1986, I had so many needles of Marcane injected into my hands that I felt like a pincushion. Once the doctor put the needle right through my hand, and at times I'd go into the ring with no feeling in either fist. Usually I needed six needles in the right hand and a couple in the left and often had to have one or two so I could box in the gym. I'd have the Marcane

I LOVE YOUSE ALL

injected into my hands half an hour before a fight, but with the adrenalin pumping, sometimes it didn't last as long as we'd hoped. The pain when the needles wore off often reduced me to tears.

Eventually I got into bad habits because I used to favour my right hand in the gym. I'd chop with it. Then I'd get into a world title fight and do the same thing. It made things very difficult.

I'd trained so hard for Grove and for the first time before a fight I slept alone. I did it tough. Old fighters used to say that sex and training don't mix, but I laughed at that one. It's a sad fact of life that when you become successful, the girls come hunting after you, It wasn't something that I handled properly, and it had a telling effect on my career towards the end. Obviously when I separated from Tania, my little boy's mother, that was the reason. Everybody who has success goes through it at some stage, and if they tell you they haven't tasted the pie, believe me, they're telling a lie. I'm happy those days are over.

People say I sometimes had three or four women before fights, but all I'll say is that I had more than my share of the ladies and maybe on occasions I went overboard. I still believe girls are attracted to guys that have that aura of toughness about them. You'll always see the tough bloke with a good-looking girl, but in the countdown to the Grove fight I slept alone. My beautiful fiancee Olga lives in Melbourne, but she was just there as a friend and supporter. Any parents with a gorgeous daughter like Olga wouldn't want Jeff Fenech within 200 kilometres of her. They'd read stories in the paper about me assaulting greengrocers, all that stuff. They were dead against me seeing her and for months and months we had to meet secretly. Finally I got to meet Mr and Mrs Doukakaros and I understood exactly where they were coming from. They're fine people and just wanted the best for their daughter. When we announced our engagement, they were over the moon.

I was very, very sick with asthma before the second Azumah Nelson fight because the air in Melbourne at that time of the year is filled with pollen. I'd be breathless after I had a run, so the doctor prescribed a tablet called Prednisone, which is supposedly the last straw in curing breathing problems. He said he was giving me ten milligrams at a time. After completing the course, I was given a lesser dosage to bring myself down from what I'd been taking.

Forty minutes before the fight the doctor got me to put on a mask and breathe into a machine called a nebuliser. The idea was to fill me up with oxygen, but it put me into Pixieland. As we walked through the 38,000 crowd down to the ring at the Princes Park football ground, my hands kept falling off Johnny's shoulders. Johnny was yelling at people: "Who's grabbing Jeff? Leave him alone." I was light-headed and in a daze.

Now when I think of the oxygen and the tablets I took, I believe that doctor destroyed whatever chance I had of beating Azumah Nelson.

Other doctors have told me that I shouldn't have been put on the nebuliser. After the fight I went to a neurologist, who asked me what dosage of Prednisone I had been given. When I said ten milligrams, he showed me a ten milligram tablet. It was much smaller than the ones I'd been taking. To my horror, I found my doctor had given me fifty milligram tablets! On the last day I broke one in half to cut the dosage, but instead of taking five milligrams, I was taking twenty-five.

I'd never suggest that the doctor ever did anything in any way, shape or form to deliberately kill my chances. He just wanted to help. I still talk to him and he still is my friend. He has apologised many, many times and even offered to go public and tell the press what had happened, but, as I have said all along, when you become a friend of Jeff Fenech's you are a friend for life.

The thoughts continued to spin through my head. I am Jeffrey Fenech, I'm thinking. Twenty-nine years old, father of one, former triple world boxing champion, homeowner, taxpayer, good citizen. Sylvester Stallone once promised me a pair of the red, white and blue boxing trunks he wore in Rocky IV and Viv Richards, my cricketing hero, asked for my autograph and gave me his West Indies World Series Cricket shirt.

I am Jeff Fenech, whose two mis-shapen fists earned millions of dollars, about $10 million, I guess. I don't talk about exactly how much, but suffice to say I did pay $1 million to the taxman after Azumah Nelson II. It could so easily have been different if I hadn't found boxing and Johnny Lewis. I could have been sitting behind the bars at Long Bay gaol counting the hours and the days and the months. Johnny. I wouldn't have fought if he wasn't in my corner. Seconds before each bout, I'd tell him, "Johnny, I love you." He'd say, "I love you, too."

Then Beau woke up. I was all stitched up, but he said, "Daddy, you're beautiful." That made me the proudest dad in all the world.

Chapter Two

Street Kid

ONLY God would know how I didn't end up in gaol or on drugs. I wasn't a squeaky clean angel when I was a kid. I was offered drugs many times, and I was always strong enough to say no, but for how long could I have kept saying no if it wasn't for boxing? I was very, very lucky. I believe we're all put in the hands of the Lord and your destiny is your destiny.

I come from a suburb where maybe fifty per cent of the people I hung out with as a kid finished up in gaol for robbing banks, doing armed hold-ups, breaking into houses or stealing from shops. One time I went to this place after deciding I was going to do drugs. They were using speed and smoking stuff, but when the time came I was a coward in one way but very strong in another. Thank God I didn't do it. When you are young, people try to lure you into doing things. Now I hate drugs because they're evil.

I don't try to hide the fact that I did the wrong thing when I was running wild as a kid, but I was always street-smart enough to have a job and earn a quid. I was never greedy. A lot of my friends were and they ended up in gaol.

I was strong-willed and loved to prove people wrong. Although I was small, I played rugby league for Newtown as a hooker in the S. G. Ball and Jersey Flegg Cups and prided myself on topping the tackle count. When I left school, I became a bricklayer simply because people thought the job would be too hard for a small bloke.

I was born in Crown Street Hospital on 28 May, 1964, the youngest of the six children of Paul and Mary Fenech, both of whom were born in Malta but didn't meet until they came to Australia. My sister Rita is the eldest, followed by Godfrey, Eric, Henry and Veronica. Except that we all lived in a couple of rooms in Fig Street, I have no recollection at all of Pyrmont, but I remember when we moved to a very small weatherboard cottage in Florence Street, St Peters where I shared a room with my brother Henry.

Mum and dad grew up in Malta dodging the bombs and bullets from the Germans. Mum was the eldest of thirteen children, and seven of them died in the bombing. Because she was so busy looking after the younger ones, she never had time to learn to read and write.

My father was a pensioner who always was sick with heart problems or in hospital, although he had worked as a forklift driver and later as projection man in a cinema. When we were living in Pyrmont, and mum was pregnant with me, they said my dad took a heart attack at the top of the stairs. His heart stopped and he was dead when he fell down the stairs, but by the time he bumped his way to the bottom, the jolts started his heart beating again. They put a plastic valve into his heart, and dad had to give up work. He was a fighter, my dad. One day he would look like a million dollars and the next he'd have blood pouring from his mouth and he'd go as white as a ghost. Another time they found him apparently dead in the corridor of the hospital, but somehow managed to bring him back to life.

My dad once did a bit of training and stuff, and I've got a picture of him wearing boxing gloves, but he never got into the ring, though. His brain told him it was too tough. My father was a hard old guy. If any of us got into a fight, he'd say, "You've got to stick up for yourself."

My dad had a short fuse, so I guess I'm a carbon copy. In the end, his life was given an extra six or seven years through my boxing. Often he was too ill to sleep, so he'd sit for twenty-four hours in front of the TV watching videos of my fights. It would drive my mother insane. Dad was always telling me how good I fought, but he would never offer advice because he knew Johnny Lewis was the only man I listened to. Still, the encouragement of my parents was a very positive force.

At the bottom of our street was Simpson Park, where I used to spend hours on end playing footy with mates like Peter Flynn and Raymond McGavin. If I wasn't doing my paper run, I'd be home at 3.30 and head down to the park until dad put his fingers in his mouth and whistled that it was time to come home. Some days I'd go without dinner to play footy in the park. That's the only ambition I had in life, to be a good footballer.

On Saturday mornings when I was nine or ten years old, a few of us would get the train into town from St Peters and squeeze through the No Exit at Central to avoid buying a ticket. Down we'd go to Paddy's Market for a couple of hours to do the best we could. Sports shoes and pigeons were the prime targets, but we took anything we could lay our hands on. I was chased lots of times and got a kick in the bum when I got caught, but I was a good actor and usually talked my way out of it. We were deprived of a lot of things the other kids had and I just wanted to be like the rest of the boys.

I wasn't a wagger from school because I loved sport so much, but I was asked to leave a couple of schools because I couldn't cope with the way the Marist brothers wanted things to be run. My father was so strict that if I didn't go to school I'd get the belt from my dad when I got home.

I started off at a Catholic school called St Pius, Enmore, which was only a few minutes' walk from home. Mum had to drag me there kicking and screaming and crying because I knew I'd hate it. After fourth class I switched to St Joseph's, Newtown and did my first year of high school at De La Salle, Marrickville. De La Salle and I just didn't get along, so I transferred to Enmore High. When the exams came around, I got one of my friends to write a note saying I was sick and when the tests were over I'd go back to school.

Being an altar boy and the baby of the family, I was spoiled. Having brothers who were well known for being tough made life a lot easier, too, and mum didn't have a clue I had developed into a little thug. She was always visiting dad in hospital or working three jobs as a cleaner from 11 o'clock at night until seven in the morning, so I could pretty much do as I liked.

I was always in the top class because I cheated to get the marks, often making kids write out the work for me while I slept. Once I broke into the staff room at lunch time and pinched the answers to a test we were having that afternoon. There was hardly a day when I didn't get the cane or the strap or get kept in. In one class at Enmore High I'd have to sit at a table in the corridor while the rest of the kids did their work inside because I used to disrupt things by talking or trying to get the last word with the teacher. Still, I liked mixing with the phys ed teachers and sometimes I'd get out of class by doing things to help them.

At the end of each year we had what they called activities. You could either stay at school and run amok doing things like leatherwork or metalwork, or go away on a trip to places like Kempsey. I loved going up there, but old habits die hard. We pinched a few pairs of sneakers from the gym and got caught.

Although people think I got my nose flattened through boxing, it happened when a kid hit me across the face with a shovel when I was very young. Whenever I wanted a day off school, I'd just have to tap the nose and out would come the blood. With my asthma and my nose, I always had trouble breathing during fights.

When I was quite young, the Mitrevski family

moved into St Peters, and if I was a midget, Peter Mitrevski was a dwarf, and an angry little one at that. At the time we had a lot of Aboriginals living there, and when they called Peter a wog, he'd chase them. He'd fight anybody. Peter is Yugoslav, from Macedonia. At first I mixed with his younger brother Bob, but Peter and I slowly got to know each other. We had arguments and fights, and Peter kicked my butt a couple of times, but we became very, very close friends.

All my life, my parents had nothing, so if I wanted to get things the other kids had, I had to go out and steal it. Footy boots, football jumpers, sneakers. I just did the best I could. I'd rob blokes like Peter Mitrevski when we did our paper runs. Being street-wise, Peter would have tried to knock off my papers if he'd got there early enough. It was like dog eat dog. We did our best, but we were always friends. As my dad was sick, my paper run was an important part of helping the family and I had a note that got me out of school early. I'd get to the paper shop ten minutes before the other boys. All the barrows would be loaded with papers, so I'd pinch a few from each of them, particularly Peter's because he had the biggest paper run. I'd sell the extra papers and keep the money.

Starting when I was nine years old, I'd get ten dollars a week for doing a paper run in the morning and another in the afternoon down near a pub at St Peters. I used to sell papers to cars, too. If they gave me a dollar note and I saw the traffic light was about to turn green, I would pretend I couldn't find the change. They'd bip the horn, but too late. Thank you.

By the time I was twelve, I was running with a street gang called the Newtown Hoods. My dad didn't have a clue what was happening. I'd tell him we were going to the speedway, and sometimes we did after ten or twenty of us would go storming through trains and buses looking for fights. If we did make it to the Showground, we'd look for other gangs to bash. If you climbed a wall at the Showground, you could get in through the ladies' toilets, and when a whole big gang of us used to storm through at once, the ladies there would be yelling and screaming. At first I was a little kid who just wanted to tag along, but soon I loved to beat up guys as an ego thing in front of my own team of friends. Something inside me was wound up like a spring.

Although I was a little toughie who lived for football, I discovered girls at a very early age. On the street, I was mixing with guys a lot older than me, and girls were always on the agenda for them. Being around, you got in the know at a young age.

By this time the youth gangs that roamed the streets of Sydney looking for fights were attracting a lot of bad publicity, with the Newtown Hoods figuring in a couple of serious skirmishes. Guys were carrying knives and knuckle dusters, but I only fought with fists. Music to me was the sound of punches hitting the right spot.

I wasn't there, but there was one big fight in George Street in the city in which a guy from another gang hit one of the Newtown Hoods with a garbage tin lid. Thinking his little brother was dead, one of the Newtown guys pulled a knife and stabbed the offender, who would have died if a nurse hadn't been on the spot.

Street fighting was getting out of hand, and when we got into another fight at Central Railway a couple of weeks later, the police swooped. One of the three kids I was fighting finished up in hospital. My brother Henry and I and a whole group of guys were arrested and locked up. We were simply scapegoats, I feel, for the bloke who was stabbed in George Street. I was only twelve years old. After all the publicity, there obviously had been pressure on the coppers to put a stop to the street fights.

The upshot was that we were locked up in the Yasmar Detention Centre at Ashfield to wait to be sentenced in court. I was facing what they called a General Term, which could be anything from three months to three years. My poor mother was horrified, but my solicitor said, "There's no way a twelve-year-old in his first time in trouble would ever be committed."

When Henry and I were sentenced, mum was screaming as they took us out of court and locked us in a little cell. We left in a paddy wagon, me to the Ormond Boys' Home, a place near Thornleigh, and Henry, who was sixteen at the time, to Mt Penang near Gosford. They cut my hair off and when I got into a fight, the guards made me scrub concrete with a toothbrush. Quickly realising there was no future in that, I was on my best behaviour and soon was in the Privileges Cottage, where I made toast for the officers and was given extra helpings of food. I spent two months there before going home. Being taken away from your family and friends at twelve was a pretty traumatic experience, but I really got stuck into the sports. I organised a football team and once we travelled out to play Lewisham High School. Another time they let me out to play for Henson Park Colts in a rugby league grand final.

With Henry in Mt Penang, mum would get up at 5am every Sunday and travel great distances to see us, but she never missed a day. If I could change anything, it would be not to put mum through the torment of those very terrible months for her. She is probably the most loyal person in the world, the greatest sticker of all time who would do anything for her family. That's where I get my loyalty, from my mum. I used to peer through the little holes in a wall of those square bricks waiting for her to come loaded up with junk food and stuff.

Mum is very proud and no matter what we did, she loved us dearly. We had a lady across the street who was an alcoholic, and when Henry and I got home, she shouted out, "You Fenechs are rubbish. You should be back in the boys' home." Of course, I'd been giving her plenty of cheek. Mum might be tiny, but she was ready to tear that woman apart. She rushed across the street, pulled the screen off the door and shot into the house seconds after the woman had locked herself in the bedroom. We had to rescue her.

I grew up in the neighbourhood where you either mixed with the other kids on the street or you were in no man's land. I was a hoodlum all right. I thought I was tough and I liked to prove it. I know now I was only a mug because my fists used to get me into a lot of trouble.

Although my father was a strict man, I disobeyed him many times. People would come to the door to complain about something I'd done, and when they'd gone he'd give me the greatest flogging of all time.

After a while I graduated from knocking off milk money to robbing taxi drivers. Two of us would jump in the cab, get him to drive us somewhere and then jump out, split up and do a bolt. When the driver would go after one bloke, the other would nip back to the cab and grab the cash. Usually it would be hidden under the seat or behind the sun visor. You wouldn't have to look too hard to find a fat little wad of bills. Once a taxi driver came to our house and complained to dad, but I jumped up and down and screamed and cried until he believed me. Later dad was listening at the door when I told my brother Henry where I'd hidden the money. Off came his belt and I got a whipping.

The alarm bells were ringing, so I got heavily involved in rugby league and stuff like that. I ran with my school teacher in Enmore Park in the mornings so I could compete in cross country runs. I went from being one of the boys to an individual who wanted to try to make his mark in other things, but still I mixed with guys that did lots of things wrong because they were the only ones I could mix with. There was nobody else.

About that time I met Tania Foster, who lived across the road from the pinball parlour in the shops at Enmore where I used to hang out with my mates. Tania was a cheer girl for the Newtown rugby league club and we started going out when she was twelve and I was fifteen. I finished school the year before Tania started at Enmore High, and I used to go there and pick her up after school. When I coached her little brother Clint at De La Salle when he was twelve, we won the premiership and Clint was the captain.

You've probably heard the stories of how Pat Jarvis, the police constable attached to Newtown who played rugby league for St George, New South Wales and Australia, saved me from a life of crime by taking me off the streets and into boxing with Johnny Lewis. It didn't quite happen that way.

Actually, I'd been training with Johnny at the Newtown Police Boys for a couple of months when Pat, who also trained there, told Johnny that I was something of a local public enemy, which he'd suspected. I'd had this fight with a bloke while we were playing cricket, and when I bailed up his parents with the cricket bat, Pat came down and I kept dropping Johnny's name to get me out of it. As it happened, I went to the Police Boys' Club with a mate who was looking for somebody there. I looked through the little window into the boxing room and saw Mark Cribb, a schoolmate I played footy with. He often stood up on the dais at school when they spoke about his boxing achievements, and here was Mark going through his training.

I knocked and they let me in. Johnny Lewis, who I didn't know, was saying it would be good for Mark to do some boxing, so I jumped up and volunteered. I'll hop in. That's how it all started. I got into the ring with Mark Cribb at the Newtown Police Boys' Club. I got winded a few times, beaten up a bit, but at the finish Johnny sat down beside me. "That was very good," he said. "Why don't you come back tomorrow?" I said I'd love to and I've been going back there ever since.

It was the start of a lifelong friendship. I love Johnny Lewis deeply and I'll love him for the rest of my life. If anybody tried to hurt John, I'd die for him. If a car was going to run him over, I'd push him out of the way and let it hit me. We've argued about things, often after people have told him I was out doing things when I wasn't even there, but we've never argued over anything to do with boxing. He was the boss, and what he said, I did.

Still, the old street fighting fires were bubbling just below the surface. My first amateur fight was against Craig Easey at Blacktown and I won it on points. I was just seventeen years old. When it was over, some bloke said something to Tania and because I was so small, he came over to give me a hard time. I'd promised Johnny that I'd keep my aggression for the ring, so I challenged the guy to step outside where Johnny couldn't see us. Next thing I was hammering his head into a concrete block. In the car going home, Johnny gave me a terrible gobful about fighting in the streets and how it was only for idiots, but in the back of his mind I know he was shocked by a little bloke like me fighting such a big bloke.

When I first started off, I was always trying to show Johnny that I was a tough kid. In my first few fights, I'd take off with blood boiling and arms swinging like windmills. I was a little buzzsaw like that Tasmanian Devil in the Bugs Bunny cartoons, and next thing my

I LOVE YOUSE ALL

opponent was bleeding in a heap on the canvas. In only my second fight, I won the New South Wales light-flyweight (7st 7lb) championship.

Every day I learned something new. As a kid, I had no ability at all, but Johnny was slowly, slowly putting the touches on me. Starting with a six-kilometre run, I trained seven days a week for three and a half hours a day. I was learning all the time and I listened to Johnny Lewis.

Having the hundreds of fights I had growing up hardly helped my hands. It wasn't until I put on a glove that I noticed how bad they were. When you're battling it out in the street, you go in with everything you've got, but when you're a boxer, your hands are your only weapons. They got worse and worse and when I won my first Australian amateur title, I was up all night with my hands in ice.

When people talk about me winning three world professional titles in the shortest time of any boxer and being the only undefeated guy to do it, they forget that my amateur record was even more amazing. When I went to the 1984 Olympics, I'd had only twenty-odd bouts. Every fight I had in Los Angeles, I boxed guys who'd had up to 150 bouts. I won two fights and then struck a Yugoslav called Redzep Redzepovski. Before that I'd represented Australia in Belfast, Taiwan, Bangkok and Jakarta and was chosen to box for Oceania in the World Cup in Rome.

Chapter Three

Olympic Robbery

WHETHER at Olympic level or club level, amateur boxing is very amateurish. It seems to breed officials who know nothing whatsoever about it. They are hangers-on and would-bes who are just after the trips and other rewards.

In football, you find coaches who are ex-players and administrators who also have pulled on a boot. In boxing, we have some guys who wouldn't know how to lace up a glove. It's about time Arthur Tunstall, let somebody else run the sport. It's going nowhere. I'm not saying that every official should be an ex-boxer, just that they have some idea of what's going on.

We'd go away and see Koreans being trained by Americans and the Cubans preparing in a very professional manner. For an Australian kid coming up, this could be scary, particularly as we weren't trained by the best trainer in the country, simply the trainer who was flavour of the month with the officials. It wasn't so scary for me because I knew that what I was doing with Johnny Lewis was even better. But how could we win medals and

Me aged six (bottom, right front) with the St Pius, Enmore team.

Middle front, captain of Enmore High School.

Aged 12, playing for Henson Park Colts. Inset, Paul and Mary Fenech, looking stylish.

Winner over David Mwaba, Los Angeles Olympics, 1984.
Loser to Redzep Redzepovski.

My family and friends gave me a medal when I got home.

With my special friend Julian Stewart.

Without Con Spyropoulos, I'd be nothing.

On my 21st birthday.

With my first world title belt, the IBF bantamweight championship.

Team Fenech in Fiji.

With Johnny Lewis and Pat Jarvis, who got me off the streets.

At the Caltex Awards with Mike Cleary, Jack Gibson and James Packer.

With my good buddy Reno Nicastro.

be competitive if all of a sudden we were given a different training routine by a different trainer ten days before the event? It was ludicrous and at times I rebelled. I'd say I was sick or didn't need to train, and then I'd go on my own and work at the things Johnny had taught me.

So I could make the trips my mum would save from her pension money, and I'd run chook raffles at the Marrickville Hotel and among the local council workers. The kids at Enmore High would have a whip-around at school assembly to help. A lot of times we had to buy our own tracksuits. But when we went to the World Cup in Rome as part of the Oceania team, the Americans, the Cubans and the Italians all were dressed beautifully. Being proud kids, we wanted to look like a team, so we bought dark blue and light blue tracksuits and sewed on an emblem.

I never got to fight a Cuban, but it was awesome watching them go through their punches. Like when Mike Tyson started out, practically all the guys were intimidated by them. I'd hear them say, "Jeez, I hope I don't draw a Cuban." It's like they were men from another planet. But if you take the fight to them and back them up, they are beatable. No risk.

In the World Cup semi-finals, I was beaten by Heo Yung Mo, who was very quick, a good puncher and very experienced. A world class fighter. The Koreans had hired an American coach for a couple of years, and Mo was the pick of their boxers. As I'd had only twelve or thirteen amateur fights when I went to Rome, Mo understandably beat me and lost to a Cuban in the final. Mo was freely tipped as a medal winner in the Los Angeles Olympics, so I was happy to pick up a bronze medal. You wouldn't believe it, but in my next overseas trip to Bangkok I drew Mo in the first round. He beat me again, but this time it was a very close fight. I improved so dramatically that I knew from that day that I was learning and learning well.

I had nothing against any of the trainers I went away with. In fact a couple were very understanding, especially Bo Gerring, of Melbourne, who was in charge in Bangkok. He'd always ask, "Son, what have you been doing with Johnny?" After I'd lost to Mo, Bo said, "Son, I'll tell you one thing. You'll be a world champion one day."

I had a lot of fun on those amateur trips with guys like Shane Knox and Wilf Gentzen. On my first trip away in Belfast, I was having trouble making the weight. Come on, Jeff, they'd say. Come down and have some banana ice cream with us. You'll lose weight easily. With a day and a half to go, I was eight pounds over and the guys thought it was hilarious. Next thing they filled me up with fluid tablets and laxatives. I was never off the toilet, but I made the weight and managed to win a bronze medal, admittedly after losing my only fight of the tournament. It was part of the learning curve. Never listen to mates who are trying to make things harder for you. By the time I finished as an amateur, I was very professional in what I did.

Sol Spitalnic, who managed the boxing team at the 1984 Los Angeles Olympics, was typical of the officials we had to put up with. In fact, I dared him to send me home before the Games had even started. In my opinion Sol definitely wasn't treating us right, and as team captain, someone the boys had put faith in, I spoke up.

Shane Knox and I rebelled over the training, the allowance we got and the visitors to the training camp at Colorado Springs who were eating better than the fighters. Ed Weichers, the American trainer who had been hired to help us, was giving us up to five hours of punishing conditioning stuff in the gym after an eight kilometre run in the rarified mountain air. We should have been sharpening up and learning new tricks. Sol and I had a very big argument and I challenged him: "Send me home. Put me on the next plane. I'll go." Weichers then sat down with me, listened and changed things around. He talked to Sol and kept him away from us, which is what we wanted.

I got square with Sol one night when we got to the Olympic Village. You can buy anything in Los Angeles, anything at all, so I got a pet snake and threw it into his room. When he saw it, he nearly had a heart attack. I heard a yell and went to his room for a look and found Sol sitting out on the window sill. His lip had dropped and he was as white as a ghost.

Then things blew up again. One night I threw a table on top of Sol and knocked him to the floor. I was ready to kill him, but Weichers stopped me. It was crazy. Sol was telling us not to talk to the press, yet he went public with claims that we were trained to perfection because we had an American trainer. I've got nothing against Ed Weichers, who has become a very good friend, but to me Johnny Lewis is the best trainer by far and that's that. Every day I was in Los Angeles, I rang Johnny for advice, so I was furious Sol would say in the paper that somebody else was better than my trainer.

If it hadn't been for Ed pulling me away, I'd have belted the hell out of Sol. All the other boys were cheering me on, and I think they would have liked to jump in and lend a hand. "Now you can send me home," I screamed at him. Sol was ashen as he left the room and I thought to myself I was a goner. Had Sol Spitalnic been a vengeful man, he could have made one phone call to team general manager Bill Holland and my boxing future was zilch. Johnny would never speak to me again. Yet when I woke up the next morning, there was Sol standing by my bed with a few hundred dollars for me to spend. He never mentioned what had happened the previous night. In fact, he never mentioned it again. I respect him for that.

When I got to the Olympic Village, I was nothing. It was so big and new to me and although I'd heard of most of the athletes, the only one I knew was Debbie Wells, the sprinter. Apart from becoming a champion pin collector, I didn't socialise much because I was losing weight and trying to rest and sleep through the long, hot hours. Go to the dining room and at one table was gold medallist Dean Lukin and the weight-lifters looking like a group of whales on holiday. I'm starving myself and there was big Dean putting away enough food for the whole boxing team.

I've got lots of memories of the Olympic Village. People riding about on bicycles, guys from Ghana in long robes, tiny gymnasts and shot-putters who could hardly be mistaken for sprinters. Competitors from all countries would stand on the side of the road just swapping and buying pins, so I joined in and collected hundreds of them. They loved our little kangaroo pin and it was good fun. I must say that Arthur Tunstall has always been good to me. He might say no to some of the other kids, but he always had a handful of Australian pins when I asked for them. Particularly the special green and gold one with a kangaroo sitting on the Olympic rings. The tourists and serious pin collectors quickly got one of the ordinary kangaroo pins that we all had, but they were so desperate to get the one with the Olympic rings that they'd pay up to twenty dollars for it.

It was bloody hot, and with my first fight on the opening day of competition, I watched the marching athletes, flags, pigeons, flame and oath that comprise the opening ceremony on TV. I was too busy with my own stuff to go to any of the other events.

"Tough times don't last, tough people do," Weichers would say. "Kill the body and the head will fall." I wrote these things on a scrap of paper and recited them over and over. With the Cubans joining the Soviet boycott of the Olympics, I gave myself a genuine chance of winning the flyweight gold medal if I could improve enough to beat my old nemesis Heo Yung Mo. Then we got word that Mo had broken his hand sparring.

In my first bout in the 51kg flyweight division, I stopped a Bolivian Rene Centellas in the third round. A points win over Tanzania's David Mwaba and I was into the quarter-finals against Yugoslavia's Redzep Redzepovski, who had won 100 of his 121 fights on knockouts. Muhammad Ali had sat at ringside the night I fought Centellas and I'm told he turned to the guy beside him and said, "Hey, this kid's got a good jab."

When Shane Knox was in tears after losing an awful decision to Ugandan Charles Lubulwa, I decided to stick with him. Just as we walked out of the stadium, a security guard pulled up on a motor scooter and left it with the engine running. The temptation was too much for a couple of street kids like Shane and me. We jumped on and whizzed away, me in my Australian tracksuit doubling Shane, clad in his green and gold singlet and shorts and boxing boots. Our hearts dropped when two highway patrol cops straight out of the TV show CHIPS zoomed up but they kept on going. When we got back to the village, Shane and I hid the scooter and used it to zip around downtown Los Angeles until we went home.

Before I fought Redzep, Ed Weichers and I sat down to look at him on video. He was a stocky little guy, a bit shorter than me, but with a big punch in both hands. He knocked people out, so the plan was to go out and box because I had a good jab and stuff. Keep tidy. The first round was close, and Ed said: "Now go after him."

It was a tough fight, a close fight because it's terribly hard to win convincingly over three rounds against somebody so experienced. Still, I was sure I would get the decision. No problems at all. Beauty. I've got the bronze medal, and the next guy will be easier than Redzepovski. I was going to be the first Australian boxer to get into an

Olympic final since old Snowy Baker back in 1908. I couldn't wait.

Redzep and I stood for so long in the ring that the verdict of the judges obviously had gone to the jury for a re-think. For the first time in the history of the Olympics, a jury system had been introduced to help overcome biased judging. Communist judges favour communist boxers, judges from one continent would favour a boxer from that continent. So if there was a 3-2 split among the judges, the five-man jury had the right to over-rule them.

After what seemed an eternity, they announced the result. Four votes to one by the jury, Redzep Redzepovski.

Next thing I'm told the judges had voted for me. Jesus. I was shattered. I'd put myself into a position to do what no other Australian had done, win an Olympic gold medal in boxing after only a year and a half in the sport. Then I get robbed by a jury of senile old men. It was a farce, a dirty stinking farce.

It's hard to say what would be the perfect system, but I'd do away with the jury, which I suspect was introduced largely so some old parasites could get a free trip. There are enough freeloaders in Olympic boxing as it is. Five judges at ringside are enough, providing they are experienced and under a certain age limit.

The computer button system they now have makes it even crazier. Three of the five judges have to press their button within a second for a boxer to be credited with a point-scoring punch. That's rubbish. Some of the judges are at an age where their reflexes are gone. How can they handle it when a flyweight lands a flurry of blows?

There is no foolproof system of avoiding dodgy decisions, but as far as I'm concerned the only way to judge a fight is by the human eye. You look and make your judgment. If you're knowledgable enough, at the end of the round you know who has won it. Willie Pep, the famous American boxer, once won a round without landing a single punch, and nobody disagreed with the judges because Pep's evasive boxing had been bewildering. Under the computer system, he'd have got nothing. I must say that in Australia, we have the worst judges in the world, both amateur and professional.

I flew out of Los Angeles early, but I still wanted to stay amateur. My friends John and Lorrie McEnearney offered to pay me a wage and sponsor me, and I'm sure if I'd gone to Seoul, I would have got Olympic gold.

I phoned Arthur Tunstall and said I would stay amateur until the next Olympics in 1988 if he would guarantee that Johnny Lewis would take me away. "We can't guarantee that," said Mr Tunstall, so I went out and turned professional.

Chapter Four

WORLD CHAMPION IN 196 DAYS

IT was a big thing for the whole of Marrickville when I had my first professional fight on 12 October, 1984, against Bobby Williams at the Marrickville RSL as I lived and trained in the area.

People were saying Johnny Lewis was crazy to let me fight a guy like Williams first-up over ten rounds. After a couple of rounds, his experience would give him the upper hand. I shared a dressing room with Yvonne, the card girl who used to whip off her top before the start of the last round. None of my early fights went the distance, which spoiled the night for most of the guys.

I had no worries about Bobby, who once was a circus clown, because I'd sparred with him once as amateur and had no problems whatsoever. I was coming down the stairs of the Newtown Police Boys after training when I passed Williams, who was walking up. Wow, I thought. I'll box him. I raced back up the stairs, boxed him and had no problems at all.

We'll never know whether Bobby's experience would have proved too much for me in the second half of the fight because I knocked him down three times and the fight was over in two rounds. For my first pro fight I got $1000.

From then on I fought a lot of experienced guys who were all shapes and sizes. Two weeks later I was back at the Marrickville RSL against Percy Israel, who was almost six feet tall. With a guy of that height, you work to the body to bring their hands down and make them crouch. Then you switch to the top. I was hitting him and hitting him and I could see in Percy's eyes that he didn't want to be in there. Billy Males did the right thing and stopped the fight in the seventh round.

Next was Townsville's Junior Thompson. I won my first Australian professional title, the vacant super flyweight crown, from him. Junior was small and solid and people thought he was going to give me a tough fight, but I put him away in four rounds.

Johnny wanted me to keep getting experience, so it was off to Fiji for my fourth fight in two months against Iliesa Manila in Suva. Iliesa had an awesome build, like a little body-builder, and Johnny was very nervous, but I put him to sleep in the second round with a body blow followed by a head punch. In my fifth bout, on February 1, 1985, I won in five rounds against Wayne Mulholland, who'd fought for a world title and had never been knocked down in 207 fights. I put Wayne down twice to post my fifth knockout victory in only two months. Before that fight in Dapto, my then manager Colin Love said he was bringing a guy to watch me who used to be a boxing writer. His name was Bill Mordey.

I LOVE YOUSE ALL

Bill turned out to be a lean, smiling knockabout sort of guy who turned up in a hire car, so obviously he was wealthy. We chatted, shook hands and that was it. Being from the old school, Bill was very impressed with my left hand. People who know anything about boxing say you're on the way if you've got the left jab. Many boxing promoters are parasites and leeches, just guys who are there to make a quid, but Bill opens the door, and if you want to walk through, he'll help you. Actually, Bill is too nice a guy. He's wasted lots of money on people who have betrayed him.

I do things fast, but Bill does them twice as quickly and a month later he was promoting my sixth pro fight against Rolly Navarro, bantamweight champion of the Philippines, at the Hordern Pavilion in Sydney. Rolly was only a little guy, and when he saw how big I was at the weigh-in, he became terrified and wanted to pull out of the fight. Unbeknown to me, Bill asked Johnny Lewis to hold me back for a few rounds.

It was the first fight back at the Hordern Pavilion and Bill didn't want it to be over in one or two rounds. He'd invited boxing's old faces, guys like Jimmy Carruthers and Tony Mundine, to a pre-fight cocktail party and too early a night would have spoilt things. Johnny would never ask me to go easy on a bloke, so he used reverse psychology by saying in the corner that Navarro was the hardest punching bantamweight ever to come out of the Philippines. I was to be very careful and get up on my toes and box. When people tell you that, you try to work off your jab. Jab, jab, jab. Navarro threw a couple of punches, but they wouldn't have bruised a jelly bean. God, Bill and Johnny have gone mad. What are they on about? At the end of the round I said to Johnny, "This bloke can't punch."

"Who's in charge?" he snapped.

"You are."

"I'm telling you the guy can punch. Box him for three or four rounds and then give it to him."

I didn't even bother to sit down after the second round and said: "I'm telling you he can't punch."

"And I'm telling you to box him."

When I pleaded with Johnny after the third round that the guy couldn't bust a grape, he looked down at Mordey and gave a silly grin. Exit Navarro in four rounds. We laughed about it later. The crowd went home happy and I had my sixth knockout in as many fights.

When Satoshi Shingaki's people were looking for an easy defence of his International Boxing Federation bantamweight title, they picked me. The Japanese couldn't see how an unknown Australian with so few fights could beat their guy, and they held Bill to ransom, backed him up against a wall and put a gun to his head. Here are the rules, they said. Play by them or there is no fight. So Bill had to pay Shingaki $150,000, twice as much money as he'd ever earned before. He was buying me a chance to win a world championship in only my seventh fight as a professional. I was very, very happy because I thought I was invincible, and my only worry was the fifteen rounds.

I LOVE YOUSE ALL

Shingaki hadn't fought since retaining his title the previous August after fracturing his jaw early in the bout, so they were after an easy fight to boost his confidence. I had a look at Shingaki, who had a 10-1-1 record, on video and he looked as raw as I was. Tall, thin and a southpaw, a year older than me at twenty-one. We were booked to fight at the Hordern Pavilion on 26 April, 1985.

The IBF was relatively new, but what gave it respect was that guys like Marvin Hagler and Thomas "Hitman" Hearns held IBF championships. Lester Ellis had just won an IBF title and now I was getting my chance. The $20,000 payday was just a bonus.

With Shingaki and I breaking the Hordern Pavilion box office record set by Frank Sinatra, I hammered him into defeat in nine furious rounds to set a record by winning a world championship only 196 days after turning professional, but God, was he tough. When crowned the winner, I flopped backwards on to the canvas in sheer excitement before Jimmy Carruthers, Australia's first world bantamweight champion, put the IBF belt around my waist. I grabbed the microphone and invited the crowd to help me celebrate back at the Marrickville Hotel because "I love everybody."

When the guys at the Marrickville Hotel, where I'd worked as a glass washer, were sponsoring me early in my career, I vowed that one day I'd bring a world championship belt there and hang the winner's gloves over the bar. With free beer on offer, it was bedlam. My intellectually handicapped mate Con and I jumped on to the bar and I sprayed him with champagne. Then we gave

Con a cake to celebrate his birthday. People have bagged Shingaki, calling him a limp noodle in the alphabet soup of boxing, but you wouldn't find many tougher people than Satoshi Shingaki. He would have beaten many of the guys I fought later through sheer toughness.

I got the numberplate CHAMP for my car and Premier Neville Wran invited me to lunch at Parliament House. Colin started getting me public appearances at $1500 each and kids were flocking to buy t-shirts with the koala motif I had on the back of my dressing gown.

Incredibly, Shingaki protested to the IBF that the fight had been stopped too quickly and I had to fight him again at the Homebush Sports Centre in Sydney. But first a sixth round win over Filipino John Matienza, who was bigger than me and was very tough. Before the fight I was sick with a middle ear infection and my balance was a bit wonky. I threw lots and lots of punches but Matienza kept climbing off the canvas. I was lucky at the finish. When the Filipino went down for the last time, I clouted him with a big right hand as he was on the floor, but referee Billy Males turned a blind eye.

I had another victory in Brisbane in nine rounds over John Farrell, a southpaw who was number one challenger for the British featherweight title. A lovely guy but very cocky, Farrell had never been knocked off his feet. I put him on the canvas three times in a tough fight. To be so utterly dominant against such a well-credentialled opponent was a sign of things to come. Sitting at ringside were mum and dad, who'd come up from Sydney by train. It was the first time they'd been outside New South

Wales and they were very excited about it.

Back came Shingaki for a bout billed as Return of the Ninja just six months after our first clash. His nose was cut in the first round and then I opened a deep gash over his right eye. Blood streamed everywhere and it would have taken a team of surgeons to close it rather than a couple of guys in the corner. The referee stopped the fight after three rounds, yet this proud man still wanted to fight on.

Japan used to produce tough old boxers like Fighting Harada, who lost his world title to Lionel Rose and later fought Johnny Famechon twice. Now they've gone because these days a brain is more important than brawn in Japan. They'd rather punch something into a computer than punch somebody in the face.

By now I was a slave to early nights, orange juice and sleeping ten hours a night in the build-up to a fight, but already I was having a battle with the scales. To get my weight down to the bantamweight limit of 53.5kg (8st 6lb), I'd breakfast on a special muesli porridge with lecithin granules, go without lunch and for dinner I'd usually have filleted fish with vegetables steamed for only a few minutes. I'd gulp down 56 pills a day — garlic pills, vitamin B15, C and E tablets, spirulina for protein, asparate for potassium and Hi Vita stress pills.

My sole liquid in the week before a fight was a special potato broth prepared for me by the dietitian Elizabeth Jarvis, whose policeman son Pat helped steer me in the right direction. Elizabeth made the broth by peeling six potatoes about three-quarters of an inch below the skin and then boiling the peels.

Almost as soon as I won the world title, Bill Mordey was planning a defence against Jerome Coffee, a flashy boxer with a 26-0 record who would have been an Olympian but for America's boycott of the Moscow Games. He was the number one contender and there was even talk of my hero Sylvester Stallone being here to present the title belt to coincide with release of his movie Rocky IV.

Being the smart promoter he is, Bill let the interest build by first giving me a warm-up fight in Brisbane against Kenny Butts, another black American who had lost a close fight to Steve McCrory, the man who won the Olympic gold medal I coveted in Los Angeles. Butts was pathetic. He ducked and bobbed and hardly threw a punch before quitting after two rounds. Then his trainer tipped Coffee to beat me.

Boxing is all about styles. Some guys fight well against boxers but can't handle brawlers. Kenny Butts was a runner, a very quick elusive boxer, and I put pressure on him. Given a bit of time and space, he could be very good, but jump on him and he was awful. I jumped on him and he jumped out of the ring. Against a counter-puncher like McCrory, it's a different story.

Coffee flew in from Nashville, Tennessee mouthing off like Muhammad Ali and when he got to the gym he showed dazzling footwork and a jab that Sugar Ray Robinson wouldn't have disowned. Not only could he hit speedballs, he could swallow them. One morning we passed each other doing road work in Centennial Park, and Coffee screamed: "You're a nobody, Fenech. It's Coffee time."

When the fight came off on 2 December, 1985, it was a sell-out which broke Bruce Springsteen's Sydney Entertainment Centre record gate takings of $286,000, with my share being my first ever six-figure purse.

With Grace Jones taking Sylvester Stallone's place at ringside, I went out and out-jabbed the guy they said had the best jab they'd seen in Australia. Every time I tried to get in close to fight Coffee, Rudy Battle, the black American referee, would stop the fight and make us break. No problem, because it made me go fifteen rounds and silence the knockers who said I couldn't box. When I look back and think about it, Battle had reffed Coffee many times and they seemed to be very close.

After I'd built up a handy lead, Coffee came storming back in the tenth and eleventh and when he caught me with a right hand in the tenth, I heard him call to his corner, "I've got him. I've got him." This made me dig deeper and I punished him in the closing rounds. As Johnny said, it was a step up from boiled lollies to Old Gold chocolates and icing Coffee was a very good victory. Before the decision was announced Coffee came over and said "May your reign be long. You're a hell of a fighter." To celebrate, I went out and bought a house at Kilcare on the Central Coast where I could go when I wanted a bit of privacy.

Mexican boxers are tough, as tough as they come, as I discovered when I went to Perth four months later for a non-title fight on 11 April, 1986, against my first Mexican opponent Daniel Zaragoza, once the World Boxing Council bantamweight champion and holding a 25-3 record with eighteen knockouts.

Zaragoza was very tough and caught me with a good right hand in the sixth, but when I came back and hammered him in the seventh, Joe Bugner said into his commentator's microphone, "Jeff's a very small Joe Frazier." It was a one-sided points victory, with one judge having me thirteen points in front, and anyone who claimed the Mexican was over the hill would have been red-faced when Zaragoza not only regained the world title but held it for several years.

Zaragoza was one of the roughest, toughest, proudest guys I ever fought. He was elbowing me and doing a few other dirty things when I lost my cool and head-butted him. Referee Paul Moore saw it and said, "Cut it out, both of you."

Then came the fight I wanted more than any other, a title defence against American Steve McCrory, who'd won the Olympic gold medal in Los Angeles on a split decision from Redzep Redzepovski and was unbeaten in twelve fights as a professional. Bill Mordey dubbed the fight Olympic Revenge. Because of my weight problems, it was to be my last fight as a bantamweight.

When I broke my left hand three weeks prior to the bout, I went to Bill's house at Coogee to tell him and he said, "Jeff, we'll call off the fight." Apart from hiring the Sydney Entertainment Centre, Bill had spent heaps of money on publicity and stuff, but he said, "No, Jeff. We've got to think about you, not what we'd lose."

I went home pretty upset. I'd been dieting, but the fight was off so I went to this Italian restaurant and ate and ate. I wasn't a drinker, but I had a couple of beers before the owner brought a bottle of wine to have with the pasta. I walked out feeling like a little light-heavyweight.

The next morning Bill rang. "Mate, I've just done my arithmetic," he said. "The exes are enormous. Can we fight?" I replied, "Bill, I've just gone out and put on seven pounds. Let me talk to Johnny."

Mordey said: "Jeff, the guy can't fight. Kenny Butts, who jumped out of the ring against you in Brisbane, went the distance with him. You can beat Steve McCrory with one hand."

I replied: "Bill, that's all I'm going to have, but let's do it. But how do I lose the weight? I'm eleven or twelve pounds over and I can't train. What am I going to do?"

They sent me to a health farm at Wallacia near Penrith on the outskirts of Sydney. The whole team of us went. Johnny, Bill, Con and Joe Aquilina.

I lived on juices and lettuce leaves and every night they'd lock me in the sauna. When I got out at eight o'clock, I'd ring the boys but they were never there. Where were they? Each morning they'd tell me they'd gone for a walk.

I'll tell you what happened. While I was lying in my room each night staring up at the ceiling, they'd jump into the car and go to this shopping centre in Penrith where they'd pig out on pizzas and hamburgers. When they came back, Bill would sneak into this little alcove walled off for nude sunbathing and furtively puff on a cigarette.

Meanwhile, McCrory was strutting about Sydney with the Olympic gold medal round his neck to taunt me. He was from the famous Kronk gym in Detroit from which had come Thomas Hearns and a string of other world champions. Emanuel Steward, who employed twelve trainers and had 75 boxers in work at the Kronk gym, called himself the Goldfather after three of his boxers, McCrory, Frank Tate and Mark Breland, won gold at the Los Angeles Olympics.

Slowly, slowly the needle of the scales dropped down, but with the fight only a couple of days off I still was six pounds over. With only one good hand, I couldn't work up the kind of sweats I could with boxing and sparring. I just couldn't get the weight off.

The day before the fight, I told Bill I wouldn't be able to make the weight. "Look, son," he said, "go home, do your best and if we come in overweight, we'll give up the title on the scales. Get as close as you can to the weight and we'll still fight." Unbeknown to me, Bill rang the IBF to say we'd lose it on the scales.

When I woke at 3am on the day of the fight, I still was three and a half pounds over. I felt terrible. I hadn't eaten for twenty-four hours. Nothing. No fluids, either. I had little cuts and cracks inside my mouth from having nothing to drink.

My friend Peter Mitrevski was staying with me, so I dragged him out of bed to go for a run. I was going to make one last try to get the weight off. Before we went, I put on all the radiators in the small room I was living in at Erskineville. When I got back from the 10km run, I shadow-sparred, did sit-ups and ran on the spot. I rang Bill Mordey and told him I must love him to put myself through this torture. With three sets of clothing under the plastics, I got a really good sweat going. I rubbed on Albolene and took fluid tablets. I took Laxettes to try and have one last bowel movement.

By 5.30am I still was about a pound and a half over. I was so close. Haunted by the thought of losing my title on the scales through failing to make 53.5kg, I got Peter to come for another run. Off we went, but when I got back to the steps outside my home, I collapsed. I was totally drained and down I went.

I screamed to Peter to come back and he helped me up the stairs. Then I sat in front of the radiators and I could feel the sweat dripping off. I jumped on to the scales and was between a half and a quarter pound over, but I knew if I went for another run, I'd die.

When I got on to the scales naked at the weigh-in and took a deep breath, the needle was moving around without balancing straight in the middle. Because it didn't hit the top, the IBF supervisor called, "Jeff Fenech, 118 pounds." They didn't hold me up, I swear it. I jumped off real quick, with Emanuel Steward screaming as he tried to get through the crowd, "Hey, the scales didn't balance."

Too late. My friends were waiting with my drinks and mum's special ravioli and I was starving. As I wolfed it down, Steward was shouting that the fight was off unless I got back on the scales. If I'd done that, I'd have been five pounds over. The arguing went on and on, with Johnny telling Steward to go jump in the lake. The supervisor simply said I'd made the weight and that was it.

I would have put on six to eight pounds by the time I got into the ring, but I haven't a clue exactly how much because I had diarrhoea from eating so much so quickly when I was so hungry.

The McCrory bout on 18 July, 1986, was the start of my pre-fight needles because I had a cortisone shot in my broken hand. Having my dad sitting at ringside meant the world to me because a few days before the fight they thought he was going to die. Everyone was crying when I went to the hospital and held his hand. Dad couldn't open his eyes, but he squeezed my hand and said, "Don't worry son, I'll be there at the fight." How could I let him down?

I set a fierce pace early, hoping McCrory might crumble, but by the fifth round my strength was starting to ebb away. McCrory hit me with a left hook in the sixth that nearly put me away, and I had to dig really, really deep. It shook me up, but there was no way I was going to let myself be defeated. To prove to the world that I'd been robbed of Olympic gold meant everything to me. I battled my way back into the fight and finally won on a knockout in the fourteenth round.

From that fight on, I was a completely different fighter. I was so positive. I'd put my body through what no other boxer had ever put his body through, yet still was able to dig deep and fight fourteen of the toughest rounds you'd ever see. Emanuel Steward came over and said he'd never seen a better fighter.

Chapter Five

World Title II

NOW it was time to step up and try to become the first Australian to win boxing titles at two different weights. I was matched with Thailand's Samart Payakarun, the World Boxing Council's super bantamweight champion, unbeaten in thirteen fights and voted the WBC's top prospect in any division. Payakarun was the new star on the horizon and had knocked out a couple of great Mexican fighters, Lupe Pintor and Juan Mesa. He would be by far the best I've fought.

    I'd never felt hungrier because I'd enjoyed being a world champion before my weight forced me up a division. When I looked at the tapes of Payakarun I could feel the fire bubbling up inside me. Sometimes this intensity is scary. I think one day I'm going to blow up.

    Apart from his boxing skills, Payakarun was one of the greatest kick boxers of all time. People talk about toughness, but to be a good exponent of Muay Thai you must be adept at using and defending against elbows, knees, the lot.

    I watched the tapes of Payakarun time after time. He

was a spindly southpaw with a long reach, a dancer who liked to box and get set for the left hand bomb he used to knock out Pintor and Mesa. The knockout of Mesa was absolutely awesome. Samart avoided about twenty punches, moved left and right and threw his big left hand. Mesa hit the deck in an instant.

However, I noticed that as soon as Payakarun got in close, he tried to get away. Bingo. I'll be in close hammering away to see if he has a weakness to the body. Wait until he feels my strength. I'll cut off the ring and not give him a moment's rest. The basic plan is to attack Payakarun's body from the outset, force him to slow and ultimately crumble. Arthur Mercante, the American referee who had the first Muhammad Ali versus Joe Frazier fight, will be in charge and that's right up my alley because he lets you fight your way out of the clinches.

Next thing Payakarun demanded a postponement, so to keep busy I fought Tony Miller in front of a packed house in Melbourne for the Australian featherweight title. I belted out a points win over twelve rounds, but I felt sorry for Tony. His trainer should have stopped the fight to save him from the punishment he was taking. For the first time in four years I was able to use my mis-shapen left hand properly.

Payakarun eventually arrived in Sydney to earn his $250,000 payday from a bout set down at the Sydney Entertainment Centre on 8 May, 1987. His managers Sombhop Srisomvongse and Yingyong Parnichphol wore so many gold chains they could have been Mr Bojangles. Yingyong loved to point to his gold buddha and say,

"Worth a Mercedes." Although Payakarun was lazy in his gym workouts, we knew he was having secret workouts back in his hotel room in which he'd push back the furniture and go hammer and tongs at one of his sparring partners.

I'd just taken delivery of my new Saab Turbo complete with my CHAMP numberplate, and in the countdown to the fight Johnny Lewis moved into my renovated terrace just round the corner from the Newtown Police Boys' Club. Johnny said I'd be too strong and tough for the Thai, while Bill Mordey was so confident he had a championship belt inscribed with the name Jeff Fenech in his office several days before the fight.

Feeling he had the puncher's advantage, Payakarun called for the red Mexican gloves with much less padding around the knuckles to be used. However, with one of his people so keen to ask questions at the reading of the rules about taking points away for holding, I knew they were worried. I'll be in there working while Samart is doing the holding. No weight worries, but silly Sombhop tried to un-nerve me by calling out, "Tonight you dead." He said something to Johnny and they argued.

While stirring my pre-fight porridge that afternoon the phone rang. It was Prime Minister Bob Hawke wanting to wish me luck. "Thanks very much mate," I said. "I won't let anybody down."

With the Thais thinking Payakarun was unbeatable, they told us almost $1 million was being bet on the fight, with Samart quoted at 10-9 on. Sombhop alone backed him for $100,000 in a single bet. Before I went down to the ring I said my usual prayer. That Samart and I will be safe. That no freak accident occurs. That I'll do the best I can, that I'll come out safely and that I win. There's nothing odd about this. My parents and I are Catholic and I'm a strong believer in certain things.

Like before any other fight, I strut around the ring as if I own it. I walk past Payakarun and try to get him to move out of my way. It's the start of me showing my superiority. Sombhop again called out. "Tonight you die," but I was blanked out in a cocoon of concentration.

I don't have any eyeball confrontation with Payakarun when we stand in the centre of the ring with Mercante, I don't need to out-stare my opponent. Some commentators make me sick when they say, "That's a points victory to Fenech's opponent. He out-stared him." Well, he out-stared me because I wasn't looking at him. When do you get points for staring at people? When they played the anthem, I went over and held the Australian flag. I draw strength from it.

Urged on by the sellout crowd of 12,000, I fought great that night against Payakarun, although there was a hiccup as I stalked him in the closing moments of the first round. A light jab caught me off balance and I slipped to the canvas. I bounced up immediately, but Mercante, to my horror, ruled it a knockdown and applied a standing eight count. For the first time in his career, Jeff Fenech had a count applied to him. I wanted to kill that bastard Payakarun.

In the second round Payakarun caught me with a tremendous uppercut which sent a jolt from my head to my feet. I came roaring back with some savage body punches. Whop, blam, whop. I stepped up the pace and could feel him weakening. By the end of the third Payakarun was helpless on the ropes and the world crown was mine, I walked through his pecking jab and whaled away with uppercuts, body rips into his now tender rib cage and lefts and rights to the head.

Round four. In desperation, Samart decided to fight fire with fire and whipped in a series of left crosses which I took on the glove. I've got him now. Half a dozen rights zapped home and the Thai sank to the canvas, a loser for the first time in his career. As he fell, a final uppercut caused him to swallow his tongue and he spent the night in hospital under observation. Payakarun was tough, but I absolutely demolished him.

With Mercante telling a commentator I was a mini-Roberto Duran, I jumped for joy, waved my arms and blew kisses to the crowd as my mum climbed into the ring to join Johnny, Con and Peter in the celebrations. The crowd loved it, so I grabbed the microphone and told them "I love youse all. With 12,000 of the beautifullest people in the world cheering me on, it's hard to feel pain."

My language problem is that I speak so quickly and don't stop to put the commas and stuff in. I just let the words roll through. The main thing is that I speak from the heart. I've always wanted to fight at home in Australia and I've wanted all Australians to share in my victories. In most cases, I think I succeeded.

"I love youse all" became synonymous with Jeff Fenech, not anonymous as one newspaper guy quoted me as saying. Operation Slowdown, a program aimed at reducing road deaths, produced a poster of me pleading "Don't knock youse selves around on the road on the long weekend 'cause I loves youse all." When I made a radio commercial saying "Youse can afford a Blue Haven pool." 2WS claimed they were swamped with complaints about me setting a bad example to the kids with the way I spoke. Some goose at the station dubbed over what I'd said. When the pool company threatened to withdraw the advertisement, my trademark "youse" was back on the airwaves.

When Payakarun got home, he went into hiding in a monastery to escape the fury of punters who had lost their money. There were riots in Bangkok, with people getting killed, but eventually Samart was forgiven and is an even bigger superstar as a pop singer and model. He's a pretty boy, that's for sure.

About that time I made some TV commercials for the National Drug Offensive. The upshot was that people called me a copper and hurled abuse from cars. One night three locals from a nearby pub, who were into drugs, confronted me with a billiard cue. They said, "You're from the streets. How can you say these things about drugs?" I felt like breaking the cue over their stupid heads. They couldn't say no. They didn't have a clue you could enjoy life without drink or drugs.

Two months later I had my first title defence at the Sydney Entertainment Centre, on 10 July against American Greg "The Flea" Richardson, ranked number three by the WBC and boasting a 25-1 record. In fact, he

I LOVE YOUSE ALL

hadn't been beaten for five years. The Flea was a runner with quick hands and an awkward style and for a while he might be hard to catch.

I was fighting for the taxman. I'd been forced to sell my house to pay a tax bill and it would take another fight after Richardson to clear. Sometimes I'd wake in the middle of the night wondering how I got myself into this mess, but when you're a young fellow with dreams and you start earning big money, you haven't a clue how tough the tax is in this country. Boxing was simply a sport I loved rather than a business. I needed another fight to pay the tax on what I'd earn against Richardson and a new house because I couldn't go on living forever at the Camperdown Travelodge. When my hero Roberto Duran got behind with his taxes, the Panama government simply tore up the tax bill because he initiates such patriotic pride with his boxing deeds.

Good news was that dad was out of hospital after coughing up blood because of lung problems and he'd be at ringside. My dad is one hell of a fighter. That's where I got my determination from.

With the fight approaching, Richardson started mouthing off. He pressed the Jeff Fenech is a dirty fighter button and claimed he'd been foxing in the gym to fool the smarties who had me at 5-1 on. I was becoming sick of these Yanks with big mouths and was determined to close Richardson's for good. He weighed in light and I would have been at least ten pounds heavier by the time we got into the ring.

With the Entertainment Centre only half full, it took

Richardson about thirty seconds to realise he didn't have a hope because I was so much stronger. I tried to make it a spectacle by chasing him, but the best he could do was hold me when I got in close. For Greg Richardson it was survival at all costs and he ran like a dog. It lasted five rounds before he finally quit.

People bagged the fight, but what can I do? They said I should have been put in with someone bigger and stronger rather than a runner, but all I can do is fight whoever they put in front of me. Richardson hadn't lost a bout in five years and was the best credentialled fighter who was available. OK, suppose they bring out a stand-up fighter for my next title bout. It might only last thirty seconds. Would the people be happy then? Still, if they want to see two guys really punch it out, I'd be happy to fight Mexico's living legend Carlos Zarate. I don't mind if I'm in a war every time I fight. It means I'll get out of there quicker.

Three months later I was in for another world title defence, against Zarate, now 36 and rated the greatest Mexican fighter of all time until Julio Cesar Chavez came along. Zarate might be old, but the one thing fighters don't lose is their punching power. I discovered he once had been known simply as The King, a deadly counter-puncher who had scored 62 knockouts in winning all but two of his 68 fights. We were matched at the Hordern Pavilion on 16 October, 1987.

Zarate quit boxing in a huff after losing what was said to be a red hot decision to his former sparring partner Lupe Pintor in 1979, but six years later he made a comeback to boost his cashflow. After twelve straight wins, nine by knockout, Carlos now had a chance to win another world title. He was an old fox, so Johnny warned me to get the early points in case the bout was stopped through a head clash and Zarate was in front. Under WBC rules, if the fight was stopped after three rounds from what the referee rules was an accidental head clash, the boxer with the most points is declared the winner. We knew Carlos wouldn't hesitate to head-butt me if he was doing it tough.

Having put on nearly six kilograms between the time I weighed in and the start of the bout, I dominated things from the opening bell and put him down in the fourth round. The fight was about to finish when I got a nasty cut under the eye from a butt. That was the end of the bout and I was winning by six points on every scorecard. I don't think it would have lasted twelve rounds, but if it had Zarate would have been a very sick and sorry man. I hastened the healing of the eye gash by rubbing dampened vitamin E tablets into the wound.

Without doubt, Carlos would have been the greatest fighter I faced had I caught him earlier in his career, but I fought him towards the end. Still, you can only fight who they put in front of you. With Zarate being Mexican and WBC president Jose Sulaiman being who he is, Carlos got another world title shot shortly after I relinquished the championship a few months later.

Next thing I was off to London to support my gym-mate Joe Bugner, one of the nicest guys you'd ever hope to meet, in his comeback fight with Frank Bruno. You can only applaud people who get off their bums and try to do things, and Joe is one of them. He struck a few problems, so he came back to boxing to get the big bucks he needed. When he got to London, Joe struck lots of hassles. First of all, there was a huge blow-up when his ex-wife Melody jumped on to the front pages of the tabloids with all sorts of wild accusations. Meanwhile, Joe was there all lovey-dovey with his wife Marlene, getting bigger and bigger as he prepared for one last pay day. By the time the fight came, he was huge, nothing like the guy who gave Joe Frazier a hard fight and twice battled it out with Muhammad Ali, going the full fifteen rounds in a world title bout in Kuala Lumpur.

One day Joe failed to turn up at a press conference and the newspaper guys were buzzing around. "Look," I said, "you didn't get it from me, but Joe's doing the dirty on Marlene. He's gone back to Melody." That cleared the room in five seconds.

I went to the fight with Joe in his stretch limo, and when we arrived at White Hart Lane, the home ground of the Tottenham Hotspur Soccer Club, the skinheads were screaming and kicking the car. Being patriotic, I jumped out but quickly got back in when I saw I would be a target for a hundred bovver boys. I might be a street fighter, but I'm not that stupid. I'm pretty similar to Mark Geyer, the Test rugby league player who is always getting into trouble. Like the guys who went up the cliffs at Gallipoli, we'll stick up for our mates to the end. More than 35,000 Bruno fans went wild when Johnny Lewis threw in the towel in the eighth round before Joe could get hurt, but I

My first press conference with Bill Mordey in 1985.

Press conference, 1991, with Bill and Miguel Francia.

A week later Leo the lion tore up one of his trainers.

Two of my footy favourites. Mario Fenech tests my chin and Dan Stains gives me a lift.

Putting Kostya Tszyu through pad-work in Memphis, Tennessee.

Good guys: Brian Doyle, Peter Mitrevski, Kostya Kszyu, Johnny Lewis and Virgil Hill with me before Fenech-Azumah Nelson II.

Olympic Revenge: Mario Fenech and Peter Mitrevski give me a lift after I'd beaten Steve McCrory.

With Johnny Lewis after I'd beaten Satoshi Shingaki for world title number one.

With Johnny on the pads.

Young and ambitious.

Punishing Victor Callejas.

My first real knockdown at the hands of Mario Martinez in Melbourne.

Look at those abdominals!

Disposing of Western Samoa's Lautapaa Ofe Wong King in my amateur days.

reckon Joe had the last laugh. The fight grossed more than $7 million and Joe's bank manager was smiling again.

Johnny had said eighteen months earlier that I'd hit my peak as a featherweight and on 11 December, 1987, at the Sydney Entertainment Centre, I stopped defying nature and stepped out of the super bantamweights to fight Argentina's Osmar Avila, the WBC's tenth ranked featherweight who'd lost only twice in 43 fights.

When I looked at the tapes of Avila and people told me how he was doing some amazing things skipping over sticks in the gym, I knew I was in for a hard fight. Osmar was a tough southpaw who had never been knocked down, a tradesman who was one of the fittest fighters ever to come here. We'd got word that Azumah Nelson was about to step up a division for a shot at Pernell Whitaker's lightweight championship, so if I won impressively I could well get a chance to fight for the vacant WBC featherweight title.

Johnny's plan was for me to take my time, but I was very pumped up and hit Avila with a couple of good shots early, especially to the body. Then I left hooked him to the jaw and it was all over in 56 seconds. I was 19-0 and Tommy Burns, one of the all-time greats of Australian boxing, told the media guys at ringside that I was better than Jimmy Carruthers, Lionel Rose and Johnny Famechon and it would take a man nine pounds heavier to stretch me.

It's a sad thing, but with only 5000 people turning up Bill Mordey was thinking he'd have to take all my future fights to Melbourne. When Mike Tyson blows a guy away in the first round, they hero-worship him and say he's awesome. Yet when I knock out Avila in one round, the knockers in Sydney simply say he can't fight. When I beat Daniel Zaragoza and Greg Richardson, people said they couldn't fight, yet both these guys went back to America and won a world title. Maybe I've become too good for my own good. But when word came through that Nelson had vacated the title and I was to fight Victor Callejas for the championship, Bill decided to give Sydney one more try.

Chapter Six

World Title III

I'LL go to my grave saying that my greatest performance in a boxing ring was the night I fought with one hand to stop Victor Callejas in the 10th round to become the first man in boxing history to win world championships in three divisions with an unbeaten record. I then had twenty wins from twenty fights, with sixteen knockouts.

I went into the fight at the Sydney Entertainment Centre on 7 March, 1988, with a broken right hand. The pain was simply indescribable, but with the WBC featherweight championship having become vacant, I wasn't going to give somebody else the chance of a title shot.

On the evidence of the lethal left uppercut thrown by Callejas to knock out Italian Loris Stecca in a defence of his world super bantamweight crown in Rimini in 1985, the Puerto Rican was a murderous puncher. Stecca's jaw was broken by a punch that lifted him right off the ground. After losing his first fight as a professional, Callejas had won twenty-four in a row, all but four of them by knockout. Apart from Stecca, he'd also beaten

Korea's tough IBF champion Seung Hoon Lee.

After looking at the tapes of him bowling over Stecca in six rounds, I knew Victor Callejas was the best, the hardest and most dangerous opponent I had faced. Still, if I wanted to become the 11th man to win three world titles, among them Sugar Ray Leonard, Thomas Hearns and my special hero Roberto Duran, I couldn't expect to have an easy night. Actually, I'd been bracketed with Mike Tyson, Julio Cesar Chavez, Leonard and Hearns as runners-up to Evander Holyfield as Ring Magazine's Fighter of the Year for 1987.

I've seen all the great boxers like Sugar Ray Robinson, Joe Louis, Jack Dempsey, Muhammad Ali, Marvin Hagler, Hearns and Leonard, but none of them have captured my imagination like Roberto Duran, the vicious man from Panama who won world titles in four divisions. He had all the moves, punching power and a great chin. More than that, he was a killer who loved hurting people. I cultivated the same sort of beard he did and even named my doberman Duran.

A month before the fight I broke my hand sparring. I didn't tell Johnny because he might have called the fight off. My chiropractor knew, and I told Bill Mordey I was in a bit of pain. I was confident I could fight through the pain because I'd done it before, and I believed in my heart that nobody in the world could beat me.

Callejas was a swarthy little guy with a black moustache and a face full of the obligatory stubble who strutted around wearing black reflecting shades and the intimidating air of a man who knows he is widely regarded as the hardest punching featherweight in the world. Well, they might call him Vicious Victor, but he didn't intimidate Jeff Fenech. At twenty-seven, Callejas was four years older than me.

Johnny's game plan was one of selective aggression, the one I'd used to eclipse another big hitter Carlos Zarate five months earlier. Move forward and keep Callejas under extreme pressure so he doesn't have time and space to load up on those big left hooks. Gloves high to protect the head and elbows ready to pick off the Puerto Rican's body shots.

Callejas will be dangerous, very dangerous. I don't under-estimate his power for a second, but I'm confident I can slip those bombs and counter-punch my way to my third world title. As Samart Payakarun had done, we were convinced he had tried to fool us by boxing lazily in the gym after training flat chat in secret.

I told Prime Minister Bob Hawke I'd win for sure when he rang me at the weigh-in to wish me luck. When the doctor examined me before the fight, I gritted my teeth and tried to show no pain. If I had I would have let down my friend Mario Fenech, the South Sydney league captain who I've seen with cuts in the head like he's been hit with an axe. Mario also has had to shrug off the mental anguish from not being selected in representative teams when he deserved it. Another league player who motivates me is Steve Mortimer, of Canterbury-Bankstown and Australia. While I was in the dressing room waiting to fight Callejas, I got an absolutely beautiful letter from Steve in which he talked about his children and said how much he loved Johnny and me. I wanted to do Steve proud because I loved him.

An hour before I stepped into the ring, I was sitting at ringside cheering on my schoolboy friend Peter Mitrevski in his quest to win the Australian super flyweight title in a fight with Charlie Brown, of Newcastle. When Peter was declared the winner in the eighth round, I knew nobody in the world could beat me that night. Peter's win meant so much to both of us. He fought a very smart fight and I kept telling myself I had to do the same thing against Callejas. Think all the way and don't get sucked into a brawl.

In the first minute of the fight Callejas hit me with the same left uppercut he'd scythed in to break Stecca's jaw. Christ. My hands seemed stuck to my sides and I had nothing to offer. For a split second I was empty of energy. Callejas gave me a look which said, "I've got you, baby. This is my fight. It's just a matter of time." I had to turn round the tide and by the end of the round I was hitting him back and hurting him.

When I belted Callejas with a right hand in the second round, the pain shot up my arm. It was gone. I was left with one hand, so I had to work twice as hard to get the job done. By then Callejas was thumbing me, elbowing and head-butting. The filthy bastard. We expected him to be dirty, but he was more than dirty. Still, those back alley tactics were going to slowly, slowly drain his energy. I wanted to smash him, but whenever I threw the right hand, it was a nothing punch that put me in more pain than he was.

It was a filthy, dirty fight in which we did things other referees would have disqualified us for, but Richard Steele, who had refereed Marvin Hagler, Sugar Ray Leonard, Mike Tyson, all the great fighters, adopted a simple policy. If Callejas did it, I was allowed to do it. Head-butts, elbows, all that kind of stuff. Rightly or wrongly, he turned a blind eye to our dirty tactics.

Johnny kept telling me to throw the right hand, the uppercut. I just couldn't, so he twigged straight away I was in trouble. "You right, son?" he'd ask every time I came back to the corner. "Come on, keep your mind on the job. Keep tidy. Make him miss."

I got my defence working, and showed people that my boxing ability had been under-estimated. With only a left hand to work with, I fought really, really well. Although I couldn't evade his head-butts and elbows, I evaded his gloves. I used the lot. My boxing skills, my evasion and a lot of dirty tactics to counter what Callejas was doing. I broke his spirit.

When it was over, Callejas came over and told me I was a great champion. I told the crowd I loved them and that for the last month I'd had a broken hand. I'd won every round and if the right hand had been OK, I would have stopped Callejas in five or six rounds. The pain I went through in the ring that night was excruciating, just terrible. At times I had tears running down my face. Steele said he could have stopped it a couple of rounds earlier, but he wanted to give Callejas every chance so he couldn't say the real winner's hand wasn't going to be raised.

At ringside Bill Mordey was saying to Don King's

son Carl that if only he could pump me up to seventeen stone ... Carl said I was relentless like Joe Frazier and strong in the sense of Mike Tyson or Julio Cesar Chavez. Carl, don't stop. He said I was one of the finest fighters in the world, pound for pound. There was even talk I could become the first boxer to win world titles in five different divisions, one more than Thomas Hearns. Carl already was talking of me stepping up to challenge Azumah Nelson for the WBC super featherweight title. I've seen tapes of Azumah and he's a great fighter, but he's never fought a Jeff Fenech.

They'd driven me to the Entertainment Centre in a red Ferrari, so to celebrate world title number three I went out and wrote a cheque for $130,000 to buy a shiny new Maserati Biturbo Spyder to replace the Holden Calais which was virtually knocked out for the count in an accident two months earlier. Six years ago I'd saved up $1500 from my job as an apprentice bricklayer to buy a second-hand Torana XU 1 with mag wheels. I worked my way through a Saab Turbo, a Peter Brock Commodore, a Jaguar XJ-S and the Holden Calais. I'd worked hard in my career and felt it was time I treated myself to a really nice sports car. I looked at some cars like Jags and a few Mercedes, but I decided on a red Maserati because it's a nice car without being too far over the top.

Despite world title victories by Azumah Nelson and Daniel Zaragoza, I was named the WBC's Boxer of the Month for my victory over Victor Callejas. Nelson climbed off the canvas to win the WBC super featherweight title against Mexican Mario Martinez, while

Zaragoza, whom I outbrawled in Perth two years earlier, stopped another Fenech victim Carlos Zarate to win my old WBC super bantamweight crown. Trinidad's Tyrone Downes was rated my No. 1 challenger, followed by Mexican Hector Lopez and Georgie "Go Go" Navarro. Samart Payakarun was now the number eight featherweight contender.

Not long after I'd become a triple world champion, my father Paul Fenech finally succumbed to his long and painful heart ailment and died. I stood, I sat, I knelt and stood again as the priest chanted the old Latin words of the Requiem Mass. Then I took mum's arm and we walked out of the church. Paul Fenech was going to his rest. Goodbye dad, I said. Goodbye. I'll always love you.

I was very, very upset when my father died, yet in another way I was happy he was put out of the pain and misery he was going through and finally had found peace. Dad wasn't going to get better. It was a terrible sight to see him sitting there drinking morphine to kill the pain.

The day he died, I'd just got home from mum's place when I got the call that dad had been taken to hospital in an ambulance. When I got there he was on the table, dead. I lost a huge part of my life that day. He was a great friend and, along with mum, my number one supporter.

I'll remember my dad as a great looking man, tall and seemingly strong. Sick he may have been, but when he got dressed up, he was stunning. He was a very strong disciplinarian, so when he said jump, we'd ask how high. Still, because he spent so much time in hospital or under medication, most times we did whatever we liked. We'd lie to him about going to the movies, and then go out and do something else. Deep down, I think he knew what we were doing, but because he often was so ill it was difficult for him to stop us. But then if we got into trouble or somebody came to the front door and made a complaint, we'd be sore and sorry for a couple of days.

Dad was always doing handyman things around the house and used to breed birds, beautiful finches and canaries. At one stage the whole garage was turned into an aviary.

When I started boxing, dad was one of those fathers we all dream of, strongly supportive without going over the top. Although he was so proud of me, he believed strongly in Johnny and would never interfere. He let me take all the credit for what I'd done because I was the one who'd put in the hard work. If any of us needed anything, he'd be there doing the best he could. You couldn't ask for a better father than that.

Next thing Johnny Lewis, Peter Mitrevski and I were invited to Darwin to help John Siriotis, born and bred in Newtown, in his bid to win the Australian junior middleweight title from Steve Peel. The fight was a war, a great fight, and it was sad to be sitting in John's corner watching him come back after each round with blood pouring out of his eye. Finally the fight just had to be stopped.

John's ex-trainer was in the other bloke's corner and when he came over to commiserate with John, John's wife started screaming for him to get away. Next thing John has whacked somebody and all hell has broken loose. Everybody was into it. When I saw Johnny Lewis punched in the head, I had to get in and help and then I saw a bloke choking the life out of Peter. Next thing Peter went flying over the top rope out of the ring and lay on the floor, twitching like he was having a fit. I thought they'd killed my little mate and raced across to help. I did what any red-blooded Australian would have done, but next thing they've got me on TV all over the country getting stuck into some bloke.

Wonderful. A couple of days later I was due to face the New South Wales Boxing Authority over a clash I'd had with the promoter Frank Axisa, who summonsed me to appear in court after I was involved in a scuffle one fight night at the Mt Pritchard Community Centre. It's laughable. My name is Jeff Fenech, so the whole business is blown up in the headlines out of all proportion.

Because seats for the fight had been selling fast, I pre-booked a table for some sponsors and friends. No freebies. I was going to pay for the tickets, but when we arrived they weren't there. My guests were very wealthy people and I didn't want them sitting at the back of the hall.

Next thing Frank Axisa tells me in no uncertain terms that I was lucky to even get in. I believe in the old eye-for-an-eye saying in the Bible, so if it's good enough for Axisa to say it to me, then it's good enough for me to say it back. I'm supposed to have pinned him to the wall, but that's nonsense. We were arguing, his son came between us and there was a scuffle, but next thing it's splashed across the front pages of the paper, with Axisa claiming I'd assaulted both him and his son and uttered threats. They also sent a complaint to the New South Wales Boxing Authority. Jesus. In the finish we settled things out of court and the Boxing Authority wiped its hands of the matter, as they did the Darwin affair.

About this time I met John "Boom Boom" Guttenbeil, a muscle manipulator from King's Cross, Sydney who was magic. He was not only able to fix my hands but make them good enough to be able to train the next day. After operations and other stuff, I felt my hands were irreparable until Boom Boom came along. It was crucial to get back up day after day and he got me through by working on my hands two or three times a day. It was excruciatingly painful when he dug into the knuckles, the sinews and the tissues of the hands to bring them back into shape, but old Boom Boom tuned me up like an auto tuner. He never uses ice and when there is pain, he just keeps going. No pain, no gain.

Darren Clark, the athlete, finished fourth in the 400m at the Seoul Olympics purely because John Guttenbeil fixed his hamstring injury with an iron bar. Boom Boom's dad was German and his mother Tongan, and he told me he learned his skills in a morgue in Tonga where a Japanese doctor cut up bodies to show him how the various tendons, ligaments, muscles and joints worked. When we were getting ready for a fight, Boom Boom would room with my retarded mate Con and become Con's second dad. He was brilliant.

Previously I'd been so desperate that I'd grasp at

any straw to get rid of the pain from my hands. When I was in Melbourne, a guy came to my hotel room with a little portable stove with which he heated up a mixture of mud and herbs that he packed around my hands. It set like cement, and when it was chipped away the next day, much of the pain had disappeared. But it soon came back.

In Bangkok I met a man who gave me a magic potion which smelt like cat's urine to rub into my hands every day, while Thomas Tuite, who works from the back of his house at Rydalmere, put my hand in wax and worked on it with three different machines.

Five months after winning the title, on 12 August, 1988, I was matched with Tyrone Downes, of Trinidad, in a mandatory defence of my WBC featherweight title at the Melbourne Tennis Centre. Downes was the number one contender, the Commonwealth champion who had a 29-5 record, although his single knockout was evidence that he didn't have so much as a speck of dynamite in his gloves. Bill Mordey billed it as Australia's first million dollar boxing match and it was a sell-out.

Word came through from America that I was to be on the cover of Ring magazine's November issue, the first Australian to be so honoured, so I'd better do a job on Downes. I went to the Melbourne Zoo to be photographed with a pair of Fenech foxes from South America, which I was going to sponsor. Those foxes were as shifty as I am. While I was holding one, he left a little souvenir in my hand.

The crowd was fantastic and it was a very emotional moment for me when I got into the ring. In all my fights, the first thing I'd done was look to where my dad was sitting and wave. Mum was there, but dad's gone. I'm dedicating what I hope will be a victory over Tyrone Downes to him. I want to buy mum a house near where I live at Five Dock, or a unit, but she refuses to leave St Peters. I've renovated the old house and bought her furniture and a car, and she's happy living where all her kids grew up and where her friends are. With the fight to be watched by thirty million viewers in CBS prime time in America I was very confident I could beat Downes, who obviously was going to jab and run. No worries. I can handle those guys.

We moved in and, bang, our heads clashed and the blood is pouring from a gash over my left eye. It was an accident, and Tyrone just shrugged his shoulder and said, "Sorry." It caused a lot of excitement at ringside. Fenech's cut. What's going to happen? I was worried because I didn't know how bad the cut was, and with the doctor coming to the corner to inspect the damage, Johnny did a desperate patch-up job to close the cut.

With his corner screaming at Downes to stand off and snipe at the eye, Tyrone elected to stand in close and slug it out with me. Lovely. With my body shots and strength, I knew it was just a matter of time before he crumbled. He was going back to his corner slower and slower after each round.

Downes survived on speed of hand and foot and had beaten lots of guys that way, but I really tore him up. With the blood continuing to flow from my eye, I roughed him up in the third and continued to rip away to the body.

I opened the fourth with another body shot, Tyrone fell to the canvas and when you start dropping people with body shots, to me that's a sign of the end. I put him down again in the fourth and twice more in the fifth before Downes slumped into a corner and referee Steve Crossan called a halt. I stood there drinking in the cheers, loving it and promising myself I'd have all my future fights in Melbourne.

The CBS executives were delighted and said the fight was the most exciting thing they'd done that year. My pre-fight plan had been to take my time, cut off the ring and slowly chop Downes to pieces. Instead, the cut eye forced me to throw caution to the winds and give the Americans the kind of come from behind drama they love.

Now they were talking of giving me $500,000 to defend my world title on the Sugar Ray Leonard versus Don Lalonde card in Atlantic City. Freed from the dieting, I pigged out on a huge meal of Indonesian food and a box of chocolate bars and felt like a fat little frog sitting on a lily leaf.

Two nights after the Downes fight, I went to the Balmain Leagues Club where I got into an argument with Peter Tunks, the Australian rugby league prop who to me has a huge frame and a very small heart. His girl-friend had been talking to me and Peter wasn't too happy about it. He said a couple of things and we walked downstairs with a couple of hundred people following us to hear the argument. I said, "This is stupid, but if you want to go on with it, I'll be at Leichardt Oval in half an hour."

I went there on my own. Peter Tunks drove up with some people, who obviously wanted to see him bash me. He told people that he slapped me and sent me home. If Peter Tunks ever slapped me and sent me home, they'd find me outside on a electricity pole, hung. I'd neck myself. I don't have to go round telling people I can fight. I know I can. Peter Tunks knows what happened and I know what happened and that's all that matters.

On November 30, 1988, I had my second title defence, against Georgie "Go Go" Navarro, from Brooklyn, New York, at the Melbourne Tennis Centre. He was flashy with a bit of power and without doubt he'd beat Tyrone Downes. Calvin Grove, too. Navarro beat a very competent fighter in Hector Lopez, the Olympic silver medallist and touted as a Mexican who really was going places. He'd lost only two of his nineteen fights and had never been stopped.

The guy was talented, but Navarro had an ego problem and kept mouthing off before the fight. When I watched him on video, I thought he would give me my toughest fight to date. If you let him dictate things, he'd be world champion forever. We heard the cocky American had to lose two kilos overnight, and he must have been worried because for a while he refused to come out of his dressing room. With a sellout crowd of 15,000 impatient to see the action, the referee Arthur Mercante had to go in and tell Navarro that he'd never get another fight if he didn't come down to the ring.

I really roughed him up and put as much pressure on Navarro as I could and soon his ribcage was covered with red and blue welts from my body shots. The old nervous system continued to play up and after a furious third round, he didn't want to come out for the fourth, claiming he was dehydrated from having to make the weight. Mercante went to his corner and told Navarro, "If you don't get up and have a go, this crowd is going to kill us."

Navarro had a lot of power and hurt me with a couple of left hooks. He was desperate and knew that unless he loaded up and tried to knock me out, there was no way he could possibly win the fight. He hit the canvas three times in round four and was a quivering shell when Mercante stopped the fight 1 min 41 secs into the fifth.

Mercante may have refereed Muhammad Ali and Joe Frazier, but the guy was nearly 70 and I felt he'd be better off at home on the pension. For one thing, he was too slow. After Mercante took a point off Navarro for repeated holding in the third, he took a point off me in the fourth for nothing at all just to even things up. I don't say I'm the cleanest fighter or I do everything to the rules, but I definitely don't think Arthur Mercante at the end of his career was the same referee who refereed Ali and Frazier.

My next title defence was a $500,000 payday against Mexico's Marcos Villasana on 8 April, 1989, at the Melbourne Tennis Centre. Supposedly one of the world's dirtiest fighters, he twice had lost close decisions in world title bouts with Azumah Nelson and would have won the WBA featherweight crown from Venezuela's Antonio Esparragoza if he hadn't been penalised a point for a low blow in a fight which ended in a draw over fifteen rounds. He had knocked out Tyrone Downes in four rounds, so I was in for a tough night.

My on and off relationship with Tania Foster had been going since our schooldays, but I could never sit down and pinpoint when we were together and when we were apart. Just before the Villasana fight we got back together for the umpteenth time. I'll try and be the good boyfriend from now on, take her out and spend more time with her.

In the gym Villasana said the fight would be like a train smash, with both of us coming towards each other in a straight line. We'd meet head on. Bang. If there were any low blows, he claimed they would be accidental. Word was that if Downes and Georgie Navarro were put into the ring with him at the same time, Villasana would be the only one to walk out. Now twenty-eight, he'd been fighting professionally since 1978, three and a half years before I had my first boxing lesson, and had won 43 of his 52 bouts, with three draws.

Five nights before the fight, I became one of those who got stolen from instead of being one of those that stole. When burglars broke into my house at Five Dock, a friend was asleep upstairs. Hearing noises, he flicked on the light switch and nothing happened. With the house blacked out, he ran downstairs to find the thieves packing my world championship belts and other trophies. Disturbed, they took off without them, but still got away with the television and video.

In the course of pulling off nine kilos to make the featherweight limit of 57 kilos, I blacked out several times and often was dizzy from dehydration while training in the gym. I'd simply have porridge in the morning and rice and vegetables at night. After this fight I simply had to step up into the super featherweight ranks.

What a lift when I stepped naked on to the scales in Johnny's room two nights before the fight and saw 56.58 kg come up. You bloody beauty. I grabbed a can of beer to celebrate. I couldn't believe I made the weight so quickly. I'd been facing another torture time in the early hours of Saturday morning taking stuff to make me go to the toilet. After the weigh-in I can really load up on the carbos and fluids.

I could see in my old mate Bill Mordey's eyes that he was not the happiest man in the world because I had gone to the International Management Group on the advice of Kerry and James Packer. I don't think there is anyone smarter in Australia, or in the world for that matter, than Kerry Packer and when he gives you advice, you take it. I'd exchanged my Maserati for a Mercedes, had a few properties and was not short of cash, but Kerry explained there was a lot more money to be made out there.

Based on three world title fights a year, James Erskine, of IMG, claimed I had the potential to boost my income to $2 million a year. In return, they'd take ten per cent of my ring earnings and twenty-five per cent of any commercial spin offs. Still, I thought if IMG can earn me more money than I'd been getting, I'm happy for them to take their cut.

Pretty quickly IMG seemed to be bickering with Bill over everything, and as I was the meat in the sandwich, it was driving me mad. IMG was trying to tell Bill how to run his boxing shows and he didn't want any part of it. It was like telling him how to suck eggs. In fairness, they were both trying to help me, but because they were arguing and not happy with each other, they were coming back to me and saying how much trouble they were having. I don't need the arguments or to lose friends simply because I wanted to make some extra bucks outside of boxing.

Out of respect for my hero Roberto Duran I've cultivated a beard and right now there was talk of my stepping up to fight Irishman Barry McGuigan in a super fight for my fourth world title, which would equal Duran's record. My goal is to capture world title number four, unify it, win a fifth world title and then finish.

Unbeknown to them, Peter Mitrevski checked Villasana's form and fitness and reported back that he was the strongest bloke I'd ever fought, but was easy to hit with the jab. Double jab him. Johnny warned I'd have to be careful, though, because there were a lot of knockouts splattered through Villasana's record. When his hands drop and he's open to a jab, he's also in a position to counter with a big one over the top.

Johnny said I mustn't get sucked into a brawl if the Mexican starts ripping in the low blows. I respect Villasana because he's mega-tough. Against Nelson, he got hit with a beauty and he'd just laugh and start talking.

Well, we went at it toe to toe from the opening bell, with Villasana blasting in the low punches throughout a torrid bout which I won by a lop-sided points verdict.

Those Mexicans are made of granite. I broke my left hand on Villasana's head and badly injured the right and afterwards my hands blew up bigger than the gloves. It was one of my great performances because I fought a very good fighter, a great competitor and totally dominated him for twelve rounds.

Villasana wasn't as dirty as Victor Callejas, but he must have hit me low thirty times and I passed more blood than urine for several days. My penis turned blue and the two things below swelled up like you wouldn't believe. I'm not sure how many of the low punches were deliberate. Perhaps some fighters get to a stage in their career where they lose their aim. Villasana certainly lost his. My face was purple with bumps and bruises and I swallowed lots of blood from mouth lacerations. It was one of my most memorable and toughest fights and took my record to 23-0.

After the fight, Villasana said in the ring through an interpreter that I would have no problems beating Azumah Nelson, so I was very, very happy. Next thing I walked into the dressing room and saw James Erskine, of IMG, and Bill Mordey. I sat down next to Jamie Packer and things suddenly started to haunt me. Bill is someone I love, and he was hurt when I went with IMG. His friendship is more important to me than a handful of dollars. That's when I first thought about retiring. It would be an escape from the managerial problems I was having, and I said to Jamie, "I'm getting out of this."

So I walked into the press conference, put my hands in a bucket of ice and announced my retirement. Just like that. Quite truthfully, I said the pain in my hands was so bad that I simply couldn't go on, although I knew deep down that boxing still was in my blood. My life wouldn't be the same without it, but I just wanted out. My hands were painful and swollen, so a spell would give them time to recover and sort out the IMG problem. I woke up the next day and the idea hit me. I'll do what I love as much as boxing. I'll play footy.

I felt a load had been lifted from my shoulders, particularly the IMG thing. I don't like to do a deal with somebody and find at the end of the day that the people are unhappy. I like to have a happy relationship with people and it wasn't happening, so I sent them a letter saying I no longer needed their services. Still, I was happy with the job IMG did moneywise for the one fight they were with me.

The Daily Telegraph editorialised: "Jeff Fenech has walked away from future earnings of at least $6 million. That probably took as much courage as stepping into the ring to face a ruthless opponent, but Fenech knew it was time to quit. And he did. He has been an inspirational role model for youngsters, displaying great skill and sportsmanship. He was never a loudmouth and let his fists and lightning reflexes speak with eloquent — if brutal — efficiency. He is fiercely proud to be Australian and has brought glory to himself and the nation. All Australians can be proud of him."

In the week after I retired I got more than five hundred letters. I pulled out on top and that's how I'm going to stay, and the older people were really happy that

I did it. Nuns and priests said they couldn't go to sleep until they'd watched me fight on TV. As a kid, my parents made me go to church every Sunday, but as I grew older things changed. I believe there is a God there and stuff like that. With my sister Veronica organising it, groups of nuns used to call into my hotel for a chat before my fights. Many said they'd get changed out of their uniforms to go and stand at the back of pubs and watch me on Sky Channel. Not only did I appeal to kids and boxing fans, apparently I appealed to everybody.

Chapter Seven

Punch-up in Atlantic City

I DON'T entirely dislike Jeff Harding, and let me say I have respect for his heart, his courage and the way he works so hard. Every time he wins a world title fight, nobody deserves to win it more.

In fact, I was the one who brought Harding to the Johnny Lewis gym. I invited him while we were in Melbourne for the Australian championships which were the trials for the Los Angeles Olympics. The guy was tough, but he needed a mentor like Johnny to bring out the best in him.

Now I wish I hadn't. I'm not sure what Jeff's problem was. He wouldn't have walked away from Johnny if there wasn't one. Maybe he couldn't live with the attention I got from the public and the media, but that was nothing to do with me or Johnny. If Harding was in my shadow, it was because he wanted to be. There were times Johnny put me behind him hoping he didn't think that.

Boxing with Harding helped my career and I'm sure it helped him, too. We boxed lots and lots of hard rounds.

I was a lot lighter than Jeff, so we only boxed four or six rounds at a time. When I sparred with him, my biggest asset was that I had great balance. Jeff was a guy who came in all the time, so I was very comfortable putting some punches together at a rapid speed. Obviously I was quicker than Jeff, so I'd give him a little shove and make him move off me. He was bigger and stronger, but backing up is all about balance and knowing how to use your weight. Jeff would come back and I'd do the same again. I had no problems doing that.

Talking of short fuses, Harding has got one in the Jeff Fenech class. People were always on edge when he walked into the gym. It was a blessing in disguise when he left because it became a happier place and Johnny Lewis was a happier man.

I first met Manny Hinton when Johnny asked if his friend could help in my corner. No problem. But while Manny was sitting there in the gym, he was telling things to Harding and Jeff listened to him. Next thing they'd walked out and with Manny as his trainer, Harding lost his WBC world light-heavyweight title in July, 1990, by a knockout to Dennis Andries in Melbourne. I believe that Jeff Harding would never have lost to Andries if Johnny had been in his corner.

Jeff Harding wasn't the first boxer Manny had asked to leave the gym, either. The first was my long-time friend Peter Mitrevski. Thinking that maybe Peter was getting close to a world flyweight title shot, Manny got into his ear and offered him the opportunity to train with him at a gym at St George. He didn't realise that one of Peter's strengths is his loyalty and that he would rather train once a week with Johnny Lewis than twenty-seven times with Manny Hinton.

I had been playing with the Parramatta rugby league club for a few months when Harding got an unexpected chance to fight Andries for the world title as a replacement in June, 1989. Because he still was with the gym, I pulled the pin on footy and went to Atlantic City to support him.

People thought I was crazy to play football, but I'd do it all over again because I love the sport and admire the guys who play it. If I had a choice of excelling in one particular sport, I'd pick rugby league as a hooker or half-back. I know a good big man is supposed to always beat a good little man, but I'm happy the way I am. I'm a strong believer that size counts for nothing. It's the inner self that counts.

It was a nerve-racking thing. Here I was, a world champion boxer trying to do something I hadn't done for so long, although part of my boxing training was going to the park with a footy. Kicking, passing, doing sprints and stuff like that.

When Newtown was put out of the Sydney premiership, I became a Parramatta supporter. Because they were my mates, I used to watch Mario Fenech playing for Souths, Pat Jarvis for St George and Steve Mortimer with Canterbury, but all the time I had a soft spot for the Parramatta Eels. I really felt for the Eels when St George beat them in a grand final replay.

I was 57 kilos in my last fight against Marcos

Villasana, but I quickly bulked up to 74.5 kilos. Just with training, mind you. No chemical help. They gave me the number 46 jumper and I was used as a replacement in Parramatta's reserve grade team coached by Peter Louis, who went on to coach North Sydney with great success. My first football cheque was for five dollars, a far cry from the $600,000 I could have got for staying in boxing for a unification bout with World Boxing Association featherweight champion Antonio Esparragoza.

Just before I played my first game with Parramatta, Tania found out she was going to have a baby in the New Year. I didn't know if I should make Tania lie down or rush out and buy a box of cigars. I was over the moon and so was my family.

Of course, I knew that I was going to cop the odd cheap shot from swinging arms in the tackle when I took the field as a Parramatta Eel, so I was prepared for it. I'm not sure of the guy's name, but when I played against Cronulla he belted me every time I took the ball up. In the scrum, too. He knew I wouldn't have a go back, so he went a bit overboard.

The same thing happened in a few other games, and a couple of times I was very, very tempted. I grabbed one bloke and said, "If that's what you want, I'll have no problem doing it, too." When this happened, the guy would quickly turn and jog back to his position and it was never a problem.

People would ask how I could be the best in the world at one sport and then go and make an idiot of myself in another? I wouldn't have done it if I didn't think

I'd be successful. There are easier ways of spending your weekends than trying to tackle 16-stone blokes coming head-on at you.

With my fuse being as short as it is, I once slapped a referee playing touch football. A lot of people get carried away playing touch and slap and hit you around. It's supposed to be touch, but they think they'll test out Jeff Fenech and if someone wants to slap me, they'll get one back. The referee stopped the game because of a fight and slapped me in the back. So I slapped him right back.

I think there was pressure from John Monie, the first grade coach at Parramatta, to give me more time, but Peter Louis did what he thought was right. I was no world-beater, but John and Peter said they were impressed with my enthusiasm and defence. I've got a comment sheet noting quite a number of tackles I did in one game. I played lock, second-row and hooker and I'm pretty happy with what I did. I'm sure that if I'd stayed at Parramatta instead of going to America to support Jeff Harding, something better might have happened.

Go one street in from the boardwalk along the beach at Atlantic City and you're in Shitsville, USA, so we stuck to the nightclubs and casinos on the seafront. Remember, I was retired at the time and not in training.

One night I wound up in the Trump Plaza Casino at 2am because with a promoter like Bill Mordey, the gambling bug is contagious. I started to bet and in about ten minutes I was winning $35,000. Beauty. Let's get out of here.

One more bet. I stopped at another table and put

down a $5000 chip. This massive guy was sitting there playing and when the cards were dealt, I lost and he lost. He got very angry, perhaps because he thought I'd wrecked the trend of the cards, and abused me. I told him to get lost and as we argued, the security guys jumped between us.

Next thing he whacked me. A big backhander which half got me on the chest and half across the face. I wanted to smash him, but security was in the way.

"Do you want to press charges, sir?" they asked.

"No, I don't. Why don't you just let the guy go or kick him out. Let me sort it out myself."

Get out of my way, you bastards. Not knowing who I was, they looked at the size of me and looked at the size of him and said: "If you want to do something, we'll be your witnesses. The dealer and us. We'll get the police."

By now I was like a pit-bull getting ready to go for the jugular. I smiled and said: "No, no. I'm from Australia. What can I do?"

Security: "Well, are you going to play or are you leaving?"

"I'm going to leave," I said innocently, "but can I have just one second to ask the man why he hit me?"

I walked over — pop — clipped him on the chin, knocked him out and was out the door. Mission accomplished. I went back to my room and fell asleep. Next day I find out that police went and knocked on Harding's door. All they knew was that a boxer from Australia had done it. I had to lay low for a couple of days.

I was in pretty distinguished company in the front row of ringside when Harding absorbed a horrible battering before knocking out Andries in the final round to join me as a world champion. I was sitting with Donald Trump, who owned the casino, Joe Di Maggio, the baseball hero who once was married to Marilyn Monroe, Mike Tyson and Don King.

Obviously I was in Jeff's corner cheering him on, but after a few rounds Tyson started whacking me and pointing to Andries as the winner. "Don't worry," I told him. "Harding will come home. He's tough. You'll see." Suddenly the fight started to change and Mike was like a big kid. He just couldn't believe the great heart of this Aussie guy, and we were over the moon when the Hitman won the fight. When Jeff got back to the dressing room, all he could talk about was that somebody had stolen his track pants.

About this time America's KO magazine came out with a list titled Twelve Angry Men — the Meanest Fighters in Boxing. Mike Tyson was up there at number one and number two was Jeff Fenech, with KO saying my raw intensity was reminiscent of the Roberto Duran of the '70s. Johnny Lewis was quoted as saying: "Jeff would die to save a friend, but in the ring he can also be the cruellest, most terrifying, most vicious person alive."

When Harding figured in a return bout with Andries in Melbourne, I drew flak for wearing a Kronk jacket, which was a gift from his trainer Emanuel Steward. After I knocked out Steve McCrory, Steward kept trying to get me to his Kronk gym in Detroit. He sent me a huge box of red and gold Kronk gear. Tracksuits, jackets, everything. Did I wear it to annoy Harding? What do you think?

When Harding went to London for Harding-Andries III in September, 1991, Andries announced that Johnny and I were helping plot Jeff's downfall. That's a lot of crap and was strictly a ploy to upset Harding. For God's sake, Harding can only fight one way. Everyone knows that. They didn't need Johnny and I to tell them.

Chapter Eight

COMEBACK

DURING my retirement of three months and five days, I realised there was an empty gap in my life that could only be filled by two more world boxing titles. After a couple of runs in Parramatta's reserve grade team against Cronulla and Balmain, I realised rugby league could never take the place of boxing. The pain of my hands was still there, but I'd lived with that for seven years.

I was 25 and a winner and I wouldn't have considered coming back if I felt there was someone who could beat me. When I was in Atlantic City with Jeff Harding, Mike Tyson kept urging me to have a re-think about retiring. With treatment from orthopaedic surgeon Bruce Shepherd, my hands were much better and I wanted to fight, so I announced in July, 1989, that I was coming back.

I'd retired for all the wrong reasons, so I couldn't wait to get back in the ring against the Mexican Mario Martinez, who I'd seen get knocked out in the twelfth by Azumah Nelson on the Mike Tyson versus Frank Bruno card in Las Vegas. The fight was set for 24 November,

1989, at the Melbourne Tennis Centre, with the winner promised a shot at Nelson's WBC super featherweight crown.

While in Las Vegas, I boxed five rounds with Roger Mayweather, the WBC super lightweight champion and he gave me no problems at all. I'd love to fight him. I got a buzz from being in Tyson's caravan before he fought Bruno. It was deathly quiet as he sat there just going through the fight in his mind. When I fight, I like to have all my mates in the room joking and laughing.

If the Sydney people supported me and appreciated me like they do in Melbourne, then I'd fight in Sydney. I'm from Sydney and proud of it, and I'd rather be waking up in my own bed each day. It's not just that I get paid more money to fight in Melbourne. It's the accolades and the way they treat me like a champion. While the people there support me, I'll be staying there.

In America, if Mike Tyson wins in 91 seconds, they're happy even if they've paid $500 for a ringside seat, but if I score a quick knockout in Sydney, they boo and say it's a mismatch. If I have another five fights or another 55, I'll never fight in Sydney again.

At this time I was offered two parts in a movie being made about the life of Lionel Rose, who became the first Aboriginal to win a world title when he upset Fighting Harada in Tokyo in 1968. Firstly, they gave me the part of Chucho Castillo, whom Lionel outpoints in a title bout in Los Angeles. No way. I was unbeaten as a professional and they aren't going to knock me off in a movie. The producers countered by offering me the role of Ruben

Olivares, the Mexican who knocked out Rose to win the world championship. Sorry, Lionel is a good mate and I didn't want to be the one who hammers him either. Lionel has been a great ornament to boxing, but he's been a little unlucky. He reached fame and fortune, but let it go the wrong way. I won't be doing that because I've got good people around me who make sure I channel things in the right direction.

People always ask me to compare Lionel Rose with Johnny Famechon and Jimmy Carruthers, but you can't. For one thing I didn't see them in their prime, although I've watched tapes, which don't give you the same feeling as watching them live. Fammo was a brilliant speed man, one of the best boxers I've ever seen, and the way he's fighting back after his accident is testimony to his courage. I was a big bantamweight, but Lionel was every bit as big as me. A great talent, great puncher and a lovely, lovely guy. Then you have Jimmy Carruthers, perhaps the best of the lot. I was awed by the tape of him bombing out South African Vic Toweel in one round to win the world bantamweight title. Jimmy was a southpaw, so strong and healthy with a long reach, and he always was very supportive of me. For such a small country, Australia certainly has had its share of great fighters.

With his only recent losses at the hands of legends Julio Cesar Chavez and Azumah Nelson, the first of his two losses to the Ghanaian a split points decision which caused a riot, Mario Martinez was shaping up as my toughest opponent yet. A big left hooker and tough, too. Mexican boxers are very hungry because boxing is their way out of poverty. Martinez will come to me because he'll probably think he has to knock me out to win. I'll try to take the jab off him early and see how things work out.

Even though I went up to 75 kilos playing football, I struck no problems getting the weight off because I did it slowly through a sensible diet. I had no doubts about going back into the ring because I'd boxed brilliantly in the gym.

My left hand went in the second round and soon both hands were up like balloons, throbbing and hurting. I thought I was boxing tremendously well early, but in the sixth I went back on to the ropes, came off with my hands down and wham! Martinez whacked me with a big left hook and down I went. It was my first real knockdown and through sheer fitness I was up in an instant, a snarling animal. It was a great punch that would have knocked most fighters out. In fact, for six months my top teeth were numb and I was positive they'd fall out. I love my teeth and I've never had a filling, so I kept going to my dentist for reassurance. Finally I got some feeling back.

Like when Callejas caught me cold in the first round, Martinez thought the fight was his, that it was just a matter of time before he put me away. I rallied and one judge gave me the sixth in spite of Mario's knockdown. From that point I dominated the fight. To climb off the canvas and score a clear-cut points victory over Mario Martinez with one good hand was a very good first-up performance after a lay-off. The sell-out crowd of 13,000 loved it, but I didn't rate it as one of my best efforts.

All I could think about afterwards was Azumah Nelson. Martinez had given him a hard fight, yet I beat the Mexican very easily, even though I'd been knocked down for the first time in my career. All I could think about was Nelson. I wanted him. A month later Dr Bruce Shepherd performed some delicate surgery on my right hand, pinning it and working on the tendons.

On Wednesday, 10 January, 1990, I became a father at the King George V Hospital at Camperdown. The happiest day of my life, particularly when I saw this black-haired bundle weighing in at 4.09 kg was a boy. I ran out of the hospital yelling and screaming to tell the world that Beau Paul Fenech had arrived. I'd always loved kids and now I had one of my own. Tania was wonderful. Some people might think that I'm tough, but I'm a weakling compared to her. We called him Beau after our favourite character in Days of Our Lives and Paul after my late dad. My first gift to my son was a Garfield doll complete with bright red boxing shorts and gloves. At first I didn't want anyone to hold him but Tania and me.

A few weeks later I was at the Commonwealth Games in Auckland to support the Australian boxers and try to help my friend Darren Clark be positive and believe in his ability in the countdown to the 400 metres. Darren and I shared a hotel room and when he blew his rivals off the track to win the gold medal I couldn't have got a bigger buzz if I'd done it myself.

There had to be drama, too. At the boxing, I was marched out of the stadium after being accused of threatening behaviour. Utter crap, of course. The Australian boxers had got a rotten deal right through the tournament and I was feeling terrible for Johnny Lewis, who was training them. First Justin Rowsell got robbed of a gold medal in a split decision and then some galah waves a flag in my face and wants to go on with it. As a world boxing champion, I've always been a target for the smarties. They know the pressure is on me not to fight outside the ring, so they hone in trying to make big men of themselves. I should have stayed home with Tania and the baby.

But there was good news waiting when I got home. Azumah Nelson had relinquished his WBC super featherweight crown to step up a division to tackle Pernell Whitaker, who had unified the lightweights, and I was to fight Juan La Porte for the vacant title. Fantastic. La Porte still had the big bomb, but he was an old man whose legs were gone. The fourth world title was there for the taking and then I could step up and fight either Whitaker, or Nelson for number five. However, if Nelson lost to Whitaker, La Porte and I both had to agree to defend against Azumah within ninety days. The fight was set for 26 May, 1990.

Now thirty, La Porte was a Puerto Rican born New Yorker who once held the world featherweight title and boasted a 36-9 record. He had a puncher's shoulders, great depth of chest and obligatory Puerto Rican moustache and gold medallion. He had had a narrow loss to Julio Cesar Chavez, ranked by many as the world's number one fighter pound for pound, and five years earlier had gone to Belfast and lost a close one to Barry McGuigan, who was then in his prime. In spite of having been in with the likes of Chavez, McGuigan, Salvador Sanchez, Eusebio Pedroza and Rocky Lockeridge, La Porte had never been knocked off his feet.

About this time, Ring magazine rated me as having one of the Ten Toughest Chins in boxing, and La Porte was number one ahead of Chavez, with Marcos Villasana number four and Jeff Fenech at nine, one spot ahead of Roberto Duran. Ring said: "With Fenech's fearless style, a dependable chin is a must. The Australian demands confrontations, then soaks up blows while overwhelming his foes with volume punching. A title fight with Azumah Nelson will reveal whether it's been Fenech's chin or his ferocity that has made him so devastating." So Fenech versus La Porte was going to be a fierce encounter. Juan and I were going to rumble.

Suddenly things started to go wrong. First of all I broke my toe and it was slow to heal. The broken toe was self-inflicted, I must admit. When I rushed to the Boulevard Hotel to do a press conference for American TV, I parked in somebody's car spot. When I came out the person whose car space I'd taken had parked directly behind me, blocking me in. The bastard! I'll be late for training, so I'll kick his bloody door in, I thought. Aiming a kick at the soft part of the door, I realised the car owner would get my number and I'd have to pay for the damage. I re-directed my kick to the hard part at the bottom of the door and broke my toe in half.

With Beau keeping me awake nights, I moved into

the Gazebo Hotel five weeks before the fight to make sure I could get a decent night's sleep. I woke up one morning feeling as though all the strength had been drained out of my body. I'd go to the gym and I didn't have any spark or zap. That's not me, the guy who usually works so, so hard. What's wrong with me? I feel so weak. Then there were spells of dizziness, but no way was I going to seek a postponement, though. La Porte was a sitting duck.

A few days before the fight, I was hot and flushed, so I decided to take a bath and all I remember is blacking out and tumbling into it head first. If it had been a normal bath filled with water, I probably would have hit my head and drowned as I was in the room on my own. Luckily it was a little sit-in bath set in the floor and I managed to drag myself out and just lay there on the mat. It seemed ages before I had the strength to move. Somehow I got to Johnny's room in a delirious state, raving on with all sorts of silly things. They rushed me to St Vincent's, gave me a needle and I woke up at 4pm the next day. They promptly postponed the fight until July and La Porte went back to New York.

With Prime Minister Bob Hawke in the room above me, I spent two days in St Vincent's with a drip in my arm. I had buzzing noises in my ear, a chest infection, my asthma flared up and my head felt like a big hollow drum. What was wrong with me? Finally they put it down to a virus and middle ear infection. Then Johnny discovered that a doctor had given me Rohypnol, the stuff they give to druggies to give them a high, instead of antibiotics. If I'd taken four or six instead of two before I got into the bath, I would have sunk under, some bubbles would have come up and that would have been the end of Jeff Fenech.

About this time Steve Lockhart, who took over as my personal masseur whenever John Buttenbeil was with Jeff Harding, found Xia Zhong-Sun, who was working as a potscraper in a Lane Cove restaurant to supplement his income as a lecturer at the University of New South Wales. Xia Zhong-Sun claimed he could fix my bronchial asthma by the Qi Gong method of curing sickness which has worked wonders in China for thousands of years.

Xia was a smiling guy who peeped through big, round glasses and had the pallor of a man who has spent six years in a submarine. I'd sit with my feet in a bucket of hot water while he slowly moved his hands a few inches from my shoulders and chest as if in a trance. Every thirty seconds or so, he'd turn his head and utter a long, loud burp. The idea is that he draws all the badness out of me into his own body and then belches it out. It might sound crazy, but for a while it seemed to work.

Next thing I was crook again and the La Porte fight was called off for good, I had further blood tests and bingo, they'd found I'd had glandular fever all the time. Then word came through that Azumah Nelson had failed in his bid to win Pernell Whitaker's world lightweight championship. This was hardly a surprise, otherwise why would Azumah have insisted La Porte and I sign a clause that the winner would fight him within ninety days?

Chapter Nine

Cheated in Las Vegas

I FIRST saw Azumah Nelson in the flesh when he beat Mexican Mario Martinez, whom I later outpointed in Melbourne, on the Mike Tyson versus Frank Bruno world heavyweight title card in Las Vegas in 1989 and this simply confirmed what I'd seen on the tapes.

Azumah was a very, very polished fighter with cunning, quick hands and real punching power. In a lot of his fights, he would fall behind early, coast along and then explode with some ferocious punching to knock out his rival. Other times Azumah would do just enough to win. In his high-pitched voice, he loved to describe his style as a cross between Muhammad Ali and Joe Frazier. Nelson would take his time and then step up a gear when he had to, like he did in knocking out Martinez in the twelfth round in Las Vegas. That's a form of greatness.

I did some checking and found out that apart from Azumah Nelson, cocoa and gold are the chief exports of Ghana, a tiny third world country on the west coast of Africa where gold workers earn the equivalent of $1.50 a day and the per capita income averages between $500 and $550 a year. Azumah, a father of three and himself the eldest of six children, was a millionaire several times over, owner of five houses, two Mercedes and several businesses. He was a national hero and famed for his generosity to the poor.

I'd had nothing but respect for Nelson from the day I watched him fight world champion Salvador Sanchez on video. They'd pulled this little nobody out of Africa to fight the great Sanchez as a substitute and he gave the champion a very hard fight for fifteen rounds. From that day on, you could have nothing but respect for Azumah Nelson.

In October, 1990, Azumah came to Sydney to defend his WBC super featherweight title against Juan La Porte at the Entertainment Centre. The bout was a sleeping pill, a terrible fight, with Nelson happy just to survive and only do what he had to do to win on points. Of course, he was holding back but I wasn't fooled. I knew old fox Azumah would be a million times better when we fought.

Already the drums were beating for a Fenech-Nelson superfight. Azumah boasted he'd be too quick and powerful, but I was positive I could cut off the ring and out-strength him. I'd make him fight my fight.

With a Fenech-Nelson fight pencilled in for Melbourne two months later, I returned to the ring after an absence of fourteen months to fight Canada's John Kahlbenn in the main support to the Dennis Andries versus Guy Waters WBC light-heavyweight title at Adelaide's Memorial Drive Tennis Courts on January 19, 1991. I battered gutsy Kahlbenn for four rounds before the fight was stopped, and happily my hands suffered no ill effects. Although I was strong and dominant, Johnny was very cranky. For starters, I'd gone straight to the casino after the weigh-in when I should have been resting. Bad things that hadn't been there before crept into my repertoire, too. My hands were down far too many times. With Azumah now demanding to be paid $1 million, Fenech-Nelson was called off.

However, in March 1991, I signed a four-fight contract with Don King for the stunning sum of $5 million, every cent of which would be put in trust for my little boy Beau. It was a jackpot deal which started with a shot at Nelson's WBC super featherweight title in Las Vegas in June on the undercard to the Mike Tyson versus Razor Ruddock world heavyweight championship bout. If I could win world title number four, I'd be up there with Sugar Ray Leonard, Thomas Hearns and Roberto Duran, none of whom had won four titles with an unbeaten record. If I beat Nelson, I'd have two title defences and then step up to tackle Pernell Whitaker, the Los Angeles Olympic champion who held all three versions of the world lightweight championship.

The $5 million was dependent on me winning each of the first three fights. Much as I loved Australia, I realised I had to go overseas to fulfil my dream of winning four, five or even six world titles. Don King was the only promoter in the world who could pull these sort of dollars for a man in the lighter divisions. However, to me the money was secondary as world titles were what I was after.

King is a huge, theatrical guy with a hairstyle that suggests, as someone said, that he has just stepped out of a bath on to a bare electric wire. Larry Holmes says he wears his hair like that to hide his devil's horns. King's fingers are studded with diamonds and he has a liking for sequined tuxedos, and long cigars and describing himself as a mixture of wit, grit and bullshit. Where else but America could a man go to prison and end up as a celebrity invited to the White House?

I'd met King a couple of years earlier at the Las Vegas Hilton when I was voted runner-up in the WBC's Boxer of the Year award. He came up yelling and cuddling, but Mike Tyson was with him, so I didn't care what he did. I wanted to meet Tyson. I took an instant dislike to the way King carries on. Everything he does is to be noticed. Take his electric hairstyle. It's just so he'll be recognised.

Because King stages so many big money TV fights, boxers are prepared to join his group and be managed by his son Carl or a King flunkey. On one occasion the secretary in King's office was listed as the boxer's manager. Thus Don King Productions gets the manager's 33 per cent as well as a promotional profit.

Once poor Tim Witherspoon finished up with $100,000 out of the $1 million he was paid to defend a version of the world heavyweight title against Frank Bruno in London. If you want a chance to fight a King boxer for a world title, you must first agree to King having the option on the first two or three title defences in the event of you winning. I went down that road for the chance of winning world title number three against Victor Callejas. Thus Don King can tie up a title for years.

When I went to Las Vegas with Bill Mordey and

my manager Theo Onisforou to stitch up details for the Nelson fight, we met at the Mirage casino. He pulled $5000 from his pocket and gave it to me, expecting me to gratefully put it in my pocket. Instead, with King watching, I put it on the turn of a card on the blackjack table and lost. Bingo, it was gone. I was nervous about fighting for King because he had Azumah Nelson, too, and they're both black. He lured Mike Tyson from his previous management by stressing that he was less likely to be ripped off by a man of his own colour. Now Mike was claiming King cheated him of $7 million from his first fight with Razor Ruddock.

With the Nelson fight looming, I had a reconciliation with Tania after we'd split for four months. I was so happy she and Beau would be coming to support me in Las Vegas. By now Tania and I were living our own lives and caring only about our little boy. When we got back we parted again, but we've remained great friends.

Before we flew out of Sydney, I promised myself I wouldn't gamble a single chip at any of the casinos before the fight on June 28. It's the old story. I could lose a few thousand dollars and next thing I'd wake in the middle of the night and go back downstairs chasing it. Not this time, I won't. I want to make sure I get my sleep. We were booked to stay at the Mirage, but changed to the Sheffield Inn because it was out of the city away from the hustle and bustle of the casinos. With thousands of people milling around the Mirage, my handicapped mate Con would have been lost.

Steve Wynn has created the casino wonder of the age in the Mirage, which has dwarfed its famous neighbour Caesar's Palace. At the front is a huge volcano which erupts on the hour, spilling lava down the side as flames and steam come gushing out of the top. Stand on the conveyor belt taking you from the street to the hotel and you pass two white tigers in a glass cage. In the foyer is the world's biggest fish tank in which small sharks glide about in the midst of thousands of brightly coloured fish.

To be quite frank, I thought fighting Azumah in Las Vegas was simply a stepping stone that was going to put Australia and Jeff Fenech on the map and set me up for the rest of my life. I wasn't over-confident, but I was very, very confident of beating Nelson, now thirty-two and loser of only two of thirty-five fights in an eleven-year span. Because he's not stupid, I felt Azumah would go for a quick knockout because he knows if it goes the distance, I'll win it.

We thought about spending some time at altitude before going to Las Vegas. There were positives and negatives, but in the end we spent the entire seven weeks in Vegas to give myself every chance to get acclimatised to the searing desert heat, which can be dehydrating and energy-sapping. When you're out in it, your lips go really dry. It once caused the Irishman Barry McGuigan to crumble and lose his world featherweight title to rank outsider Steve Cruz. My fight would be at 6.30pm under a canopy in the carpark of the Mirage hotel, but it still would be very hot. I'll have to drink water between rounds, which is something I don't usually do.

With Mike Tyson baby-sitting Beau and tossing around a few Greek words Con taught him, I got stuck into the sparring with Greg Haugen, who had been stripped of the world junior welterweight title after causing a huge upset by becoming the first man to beat the flamboyant Hector "Macho" Comacho. Traces of marijuana were found in his drug test. Haugen approached me at the Virgil Hill versus Thomas Hearns fight and said, "There are too many black champions. I want to help you." I couldn't believe my luck because Greg gave me some fantastic boxing.

Even though Don King was describing me as a mini Mike Tyson, the local media low-balled the fight, calling me Jeff French or Jeff Fennick. Bill Mordey blew his top, but I'm calmer than I used to be and took it in my stride. I don't care what they call me because I'm getting paid and I'll be coming home with the championship belt. For once I had no weight worries and I was reading a biography of Muhammad Ali for inspiration. The time just dragged and dragged, with Johnny saying that on a fun scale, we might as well have been in the Gulf fighting Saddam Hussein.

One day a couple of weeks before the fight I self-destructed. The hot desert wind was blowing so hard that if you walked in it, it pushed you backwards. So what did I do? I did the Jeff Fenech macho bit at a circuit Peter Mitrevski and I mapped out in the hills around a running track in a big park. We'd run up and down a hill, do a lap, up and down another hill and another lap. Hill work and sprint work for about half an hour. That morning Tyson's trainer Richie Giachetti was there with some of his boxers and I wanted to show that the way I run was superior to them. I succeeded, but nearly killed myself doing it in the high winds and when I got back to the hotel I was as sick as a dog. It burned me out completely. From that day onwards I was very, very flat and my training workouts were shockers.

In the last day of training, we took a busload of people out to Razor Ruddock's gym in a ghetto to watch. Press, supporters, that kind of stuff and the place was full up. Instead of the hard stuff Johnny usually gives me, he put me through this really sharp little workout.

It was over in a couple of minutes, but it made me look a million dollars. People were clapping and saying how good I was, but I knew deep down that Johnny had fooled everybody. Except me, that is. He said, "Jeff, that was brilliant." But I knew. I knew what Johnny had done. I knew how I'd been training. It was a ploy he used to use on me when I was a kid to make me feel everything was alright. I knew things weren't right this time, but I agreed with him because he is so good at what he does.

It was hot on the day of the fight, but I like the heat. All my boxing career I trained in that hot little gym at Newtown with the sweat gear on, so it was no problem. From the day I had that brain explosion and did the run, the way I felt, the way I trained wasn't as good as I would have liked, but I still was very confident I could beat Azumah Nelson. Not over-confident because I knew he was a great fighter with a great punch, but at that stage nobody could hurt me. The Las Vegas bookies quoted me at 6-4 on, but in the seven weeks since we got there Johnny had kept saying that we had to win clearly because he was scared about what can happen over there. I told him not to worry. I'd had tremendous support from back home, with hundreds of good luck phone calls and messages from Prime Minister Bob Hawke down.

We changed in a caravan at the back of the Mirage which I shared with Riddick Bowe, who was on the undercard. "Go, Bowe, go," his trainers chanted before he went down to the ring. Little did any of us dream that one day he would become the heavyweight champion. Johnny Lewis, Peter Mitrevski, Eddie Younan, Theo, John Guttenbeil, Con, Ed Weichers, who'd flown in from Colorado to help Johnny, and all the team were there. I was very keyed up and excited. It was destiny day, make or break, a chance to put myself up there with Australian sporting heroes like Sir Donald Bradman and Dawn Fraser. I knew I could do it.

It was a long hike down to the ring and once I climbed through the ropes I just couldn't wait. Basketball star Michael Jordan, Clint Eastwood, Bill Cosby, Bruce Willis and Demi Moore were among those sitting up front. I kept circling the ring as I always did, not looking at Azumah, the man who was barring my way to world title number four. The bell rang, I kissed Johnny and said I loved him. Crunch time.

Always in the first round I try to put pressure on people and try to work them out. I got caught with a couple of punches, but whatever Azumah did, I thought I replied. It was a nothing round, but maybe because Nelson was the champion and people thought he hit me with a couple of cleaner punches, he may have won the round.

The second round was much the same, with Azumah catching me with a couple of shots towards the end of the round. "What's this Aussie doing?" asked the commentators. "He's just standing there letting Nelson have his own way." I was simply seeing what he could dish out and winding up ready to give Azumah something back. Maybe Nelson did win the first two rounds, but in no way, shape or form did he give me a beating.

In the third round we got into a neutral corner and stayed there for a long time, punching, working away and probing for an opening. Azumah made no attempt to escape because he loves fighting off the ropes. He thought he would out-fight me, out-strength me the same as he'd done everyone else. Little did he know that I'm a good ropes fighter, too. If I can get a guy's back on the ropes, I'll work there for as long as I can. With lots of Nelson's punches hitting my arms, I dug in and fired home a lot more blows than he did.

We were back in a corner in the fourth round and the same thing happened in the fifth. We were stuck there as if held by a magnet and could have fought it out in a telephone box rather than a boxing ring. If Azumah hit me with three or four or even eight punches in a row, I'd come straight back with twenty better blows.

We seemed to be on the ropes forever because it was an ego thing with both of us. Azumah thought he'd kill me there because he'd cleaned up practically every guy he'd fought on the ropes. He liked you to work early, then Azumah backs you off and puts you on the ropes where he'd wipe you out. He couldn't do it to Jeff Fenech, though. I'm good at rocking from side to side, evading and catching punches on my arms and I did just that.

After a couple of hard rounds when we stayed in the corner on the ropes, the fight changed and I got on top. If the old Jeff Fenech had been in there, I would have swallowed up Azumah then and there but I hadn't prepared for the fight as I would have liked.

Although I didn't dominate to the stage where there were any 10-8 rounds, I felt I was in total control for the rest of the fight. There were a couple of close ones when Nelson fought back, but I could feel the energy draining from him, slowly but surely. I'm not a one-punch knockout artist, rather a volume puncher who works hard.

By the end of the ninth Azumah was so exhausted that his trainer Buffalo Martinez did the right thing by his man and slipped Nelson's mouthguard into his pocket and gave him an extra 60 seconds to recover. I couldn't believe it. It was like the famous time Angelo Dundee cut open Muhammad Ali's glove to give him a breather after he was smashed to the canvas by Henry Cooper's left hook in London.

With the crowd jeering and booing and calling for the fight to get underway, Azumah was man enough to tell referee Joe Cortez, "Forget about my mouthguard. Let me rumble." When this happened, the mouthguard suddenly appeared from his trainer's pocket.

I poured on the pressure and with twenty seconds left in the fight, I tagged him with a volley of punches that buckled Nelson's knees. With three seconds to go in the twelveth, Nelson was out on his feet. When the bell sounded, I held him up and if I'd had another thirty seconds, I'd have knocked him out. If the bout had been over the old championship distance of fifteen rounds, Azumah wouldn't have lasted half of another round.

I thought it was close after a furious fight, but there was no way in the world I wasn't going to be world champion for the fourth time. Johnny jumped into the ring and was ecstatic, kissing me and saying, "We've won it. We've won it." I stood there waiting for the announcement that Jeff Fenech, of Australia, had created another page of boxing history. Then those words, split decision. I felt sick to the stomach. Come on, it's bullshit. Maybe one of the judges was going to let Azumah go out with a bit of glory after a hard fight, a tough fight but I was the winner.

Judge Jerry Roth votes 115-113 for Jeff Fenech. You beauty. Judge Miguel Donate votes 116-112 for Azumah Nelson. Did he only watch one fighter? I can't believe it. Jesus, I hope he's got a conscience. Is it the Los Angeles Olympics all over again? Still, I'll be happy to cop a split verdict. But judge Dave Moretti votes 114-114. Anger then tears. I'm having a nightmare. I screamed at Johnny. "We're not the champion. We're not the champion."

Next thing that man Don King is trying to put his arm round me. With the dollar signs in his eyes and the cash register ticking over in his brain, he said, "Don't worry. There will be a re-match." If you read my lips, you'll know what I told that scumbag.

Azumah Nelson is a great sportsman and with a chorus of boos coming from the crowd, he came up and said, "You are a great champion. You are tough. If you want a re-match, I will give it to you." I mean, Azumah has won a lot of great fights and still is a great fighter, but this time he knew he had had his backside ripped. I want a re-match, but only in Australia. I will never fight in America again. You hear all these stories about the fight game being corrupt and now it's happened to me.

After he'd beaten Razor Ruddock, my friend Mike Tyson, who had watched the fight on a monitor in his dressing room, was in tears when he told me I had been robbed. "It was a great fight and you won it, little champ," he said. Calling for an investigation into what happened, Don King's rival promoter Bob Arum said, "They ought to be arrested. The Aussie kid won nine rounds in a one-sided fight. They are crooks and I'm outraged about it," At home, even Jeff Harding was calling it highway robbery.

The fight grossed over $1 million for Sky Channel in Australia, being shown in such outposts as Humpty Doo in the Northern Territory and the Spinifex Hotel in Derby, Western Australia. Within seconds of the fight ending, one publican called Sky Channel to say, "I've got twenty-two guys here ready to riot. Who can I call in Las Vegas to protest?"

As far as I was concerned, my contract with King was over because it was a jackpot one dependent upon me winning each fight. Well, I hadn't won this one. In the eyes of the judges, it was a draw. I don't care about the money. Now I don't have to play games and be Don King's puppet any more.

It was nearly midnight when I got back to my room. When I sat and watched a tape of the fight, I realised how easily I'd won it. What more could I have done? I'm convinced I won ten rounds, and I could hear

Martinez imploring a tiring Azumah in the corner, "This guy is a bullshit guy. A bullshit guy, God dammit." Buffalo, we know who the bullshit guy is. I had no trust in boxing any more. It's corrupt, life is corrupt, everything is corrupt. I felt empty. Truly, I felt like a loser. I couldn't wait to get home.

The Sydney Telegraph Mirror editorialised: "If there is one thing every Australian expects and demands, it is to be given a fair go. Sadly these ideals took a bloody battering in Las Vegas; a battering as severe as that handed out by Jeff Fenech to Azumah Nelson. Let the little champion stay in Australia and have the nation in his corner as he bids to claim what is rightly his in a return clash with Nelson in Melbourne."

The Australian's editorial said: "Is Fenech destined to join Les Darcy and Phar Lap as another mighty Aussie done down by the scheming Yanks? Judging by the outcry of the last few days, it unhappily seems so." Phar Lap and Les Darcy didn't make it back to Australia. At least we did.

There wasn't one American I struck after the fight who didn't tell me I won or that I got robbed or what a great fighter I was. When I got to Los Angeles they were bipping the horn as I walked down the street. I knew I would have got a great welcome back to Sydney if I'd beaten Azumah to win my fourth world title, but people from Bob Hawke down seemed to get behind me even more because I got robbed in Las Vegas. Johnny Lewis said, "Why do we need America? Australia is just crying out for a super hero. I think Jeff Fenech is the most important person in the nation."

I remember every punch of that fight because it was something that turned my whole life around. It turned me from someone who loved the sport of boxing to hating it. It might sound crazy to hate something that gave you millions of dollars, but it robbed me of a dream I'd trained for all my life. When that happens, you become bitter. It's history now, and I try to put that fight out of my mind, but people keep bringing it up.

Although I'm not saying I love the guy, when I sat down and thought about it, it sunk in that I shouldn't be blaming Don King for the draw. What did he have to gain? I was white, unbeaten, five years younger than Azumah Nelson, a genuine drawcard and under contract to him for three more fights. Now I was in a position to break that contract. Instead, King was left with a thirty-two-year-old black guy at the end of his career who had never been a crowd puller.

It was the judges who brought me undone. I didn't speak to them afterwards and I didn't want to talk to guys who play with people's hearts and emotions. Maybe Donate and Moretti wanted Azumah to win. Perhaps they thought he was a better fighter than me and watched only Azumah. They should never be allowed to judge again, particularly as America Today gave the judging panel the Three Blind Mice Award for 1991.

I feel the sport is run by imposters, by people who don't know what they are doing. You'll see a one-sided fight and the guy will get it by a point or two. I've seen it a hundred times. What fight were the judges watching? Were they paying too much attention to the card girl? Their eyes certainly weren't on the fight I was watching.

I'd like to see fifty old fighters recruited to become judges, but maybe they wouldn't be able to do the job either.

Next thing Jose Sulaiman, president of the World Boxing Council, announces from Mexico City that he'd scored me the winner by two points. Then he claimed Miguel Donate, the Puerto Rican judge who'd voted for Nelson by four points, was a man of integrity who'd simply had an off night and perhaps preferred the boxer to the puncher. Sulaiman scoffed at suggestions that his friend Don King had influenced the result, claiming that Jerry Roth, the judge who scored me the winner, was a close friend of King. I just hope Donate and Moretti realise they have taken a huge part of my life away.

Because of the criticism of his judging and Sulaiman's claim that I won the fight, Donate resigned from the WBC, saying "I am a religious, honest man with a lot of friends in boxing. I will miss them, but it is not worth the controversy, hassles and accusations that have come from this fight. Nelson won the fight because he was the more accurate, stronger puncher. Not like the windmill-type action of Fenech."

Sulaiman said an inquiry would be held into Nelson's "lost" mouthguard, claiming he was outraged by the irresponsible and careless way Martinez pocketed it. So what? That's not going to change what happened to me in Las Vegas.

Next thing Don King has bobbed up on 2KY radio saying that as a fan, he thought I won, that I fought a masterful fight and that I was magnificent. King said in spite of the vilification, allegations and castigation I had heaped upon him, he still loved me, but that I had to learn to take the bitter with the sweet. Ray Warren then got on the line to Ghana, from where Azumah claimed that only because I was white did they give me a draw. He said he was happy to come to Australia for a re-match without King being involved, but King shot back that Azumah Nelson would not fight here without him being involved.

Donate mightn't have been impressed, but the critics in America loved me. Ring magazine, the bible of boxing, ranked me the seventh best fighter in the world in any division, while KO magazine put Mike Tyson and me on the cover under the heading, "The Nelson-Fenech robbery." KOs Steve Farhood said, "Miguel Donate and Dave Moretti did what Nelson failed to do — they hurt Fenech, cutting him to the bone." At the end of the year, the New York Times ranked me number eight in the world pound for pound, with Phil Berger describing me as "tough and somewhat primitive, but with his own crude art. Recipient of the worst judges' decision of 1991; a draw against Azumah Nelson."

Chapter Ten

Azumah II

ON the night I was robbed of my fourth world title in Las Vegas, my manager Theo Onisforou approached Don King and said: "Our contract is at an end." To which King replied, "Come on, Theo, we'll sort it out."

King's next move was to tell Theo that if he was wrong and the contract still was on foot, I wouldn't get a re-match with Azumah Nelson under any circumstances. Theo countered by getting a tape made of the various comments from the commentators and sending it to Jose Sulaiman, the autocratic president of the World Boxing Council.

Sulaiman thankfully shrugged off my bad-mouthing of the WBC and supported me by publicly criticising judge Miguel Donate, who had scored Azumah the winner, and ordering his WBC committee to give a unanimous vote for a re-match with Nelson.

It was like a game of chess. With King's threat losing its thunder, he agreed to Fenech-Nelson II providing there was a 75-25 per cent purse split Azumah's way. Theo then said I would go to the rival World Boxing Association, which immediately offered me the number one rating and a promise of a title shot with their champion Hector Lopez.

Next thing his lawyers backed down over King's four-fight contract, largely because it became void if I didn't win and because Theo had been smart enough to have it written according to Australian law, which meant any dispute couldn't be resolved by an American court. King's next move was to offer me a new four-fight deal worth $10 million.

By now Theo, Bill Mordey and I were quite satisfied that King had in no way connived to rob me of a fourth world title in Las Vegas because if I'd won, he would have had a potential superstar contracted to him for three fights for a maximum payout of $4 million.

Knowing Theo was prepared to take me to the WBA, King came up with a one fight, no option deal from which I would receive, with a percentage of TV rights, $2 million for a return clash with Azumah Nelson, even though I was the challenger. Unbelievable. This sort of money put me into the Sugar Ray Leonard versus Thomas Hearns bracket. The fight was set for Melbourne on March 1, 1991, with Nelson to get $1 million, exactly half what I was being paid.

Another ace in Theo's hand was that at the time King's only major drawcards were Mike Tyson and Julio Cesar Chavez, with a very strong possibility of Tyson going to gaol. Chavez is not over-popular in America because he doesn't speak English, so King was desperate to get me.

While Theo was in New York playing hardball with King, Sulaiman came to the rescue. He said Pernell

Whitaker was about to vacate the lightweight championship and step up a division for a superfight with Chavez, so if Fenech- Nelson II fell through, he would give me a one or two ranking so I could fight for the vacant title. So much for the theory that King had Sulaiman in his pocket.

Theo enjoyed playing his little games with King over the negotiating table; in fact, he grew to like Don very much. One night over dinner, King said to him, "I'm worth $500 million, and one day I want to be worth a billion dollars." A lot of it is ego, too, with King wanting to have as many champions in his stable as he can.

Following that brilliant bit of negotiating by Theo, I was given a warm-up fight with Argentina's Miguel Francia, ranked fifth by the WBC, at the Melbourne Tennis Centre on 13 September, 1991. The chef at the Bryson Hotel caught me a good shot just before we left for the arena. I rang the kitchen and asked for an energy snack of a toasted banana and peanut butter sandwich, with instructions that the banana must be ripe and the bread white. The chef rang back to inquire whether I wanted the peanut butter smooth or crunchy.

I'm told Francia hadn't expected to last more than four or five rounds, but he stuck at it for ten bruising rounds from which I was a clear-cut winner. Francia held all night, but I fought like I trained — bloody awful. My hands were a little sore, but alright. One ringsider said they should have armed Francia and I with a broken bottle each and turned us loose in a darkened alley somewhere.

Eventually Princes Park in Melbourne was settled

as the venue for Fenech-Nelson II and the date set at 1 March, 1992. If I won, I'd step up immediately and bid for world title number five by fighting for the WBC lightweight crown soon to be vacated by Pernell Whitaker, with Korea's Chil-Sing Chung in the other corner.

In November, the world amateur championships came to Sydney, with the stand-out boxer being the Soviet Union's Kostya Tszyu, whose hand speed, balance, timing and combinations made him a great, great talent. Little did we know that within a week Kostya would announce he was turning his back on a certain gold medal at the Barcelona Olympics to join the Johnny Lewis team and be promoted by Bill Mordey.

I wanted Richard Steele to referee the fight, but the WBC people said no, Fenech-Nelson II will be a nice retirement present for Arthur Mercante. I was aghast. If they wanted to pension old Arthur off with a nice holiday, they should have sent him to a resort. He was nearly seventy and couldn't possibly be as quick and sharp as Steele.

When I got to Melbourne the hay fever hit me. I was put on a course of anti-biotics and had to stop running in the park because the air was so full of pollen. Instead I got up at 5am each day, pulled on a beanie or balaclava and ran through the deserted city streets with Peter Mitrevski.

After spending seven weeks at a training camp in Spain, Azumah flew in wearing as much gold jewellery as Sammy Davis Jr and claimed he had been in hospital for two days with malaria in the countdown to our fight in

Las Vegas. He pledged to die in the ring rather than disappoint his fans back in Ghana. With Melbourne in the grip of Fenech fever, the fight was reaching almost the proportions of a Melbourne Cup or AFL grand final.

Nelson is a great puncher, a great boxer, he's clever, he's fast and by far the greatest fighter I've fought. He's got tons of pride, too. Every time I did something in Las Vegas, Azumah tried to do it better. He's got a whole lot of pluses, but I believe I can turn them into minuses. If Azumah Nelson is Superman, then I'm the kryptonite.

Azumah knows he can't stand there and fight with me. He's a classy boxer and I think he'll be up on his toes trying to outjab me and outpoint me. If I make a mistake, he'll try and capitalise on it. Look, if there had been thirteen rounds in Las Vegas, ask Azumah where he would be today. He'd be in retirement because that's where I would have put him in round thirteen. It was twelve rounds, so that's history. With the whole country in my corner, how can I fail?

Beating Nelson will put me up with the greatest Australian sportspeople ever. I want to be in the history books and I feel that after this fight they'll be talking about me in those terms. I know there will be a million people around Australia throwing every punch with me and that makes me very proud.

I soon found out I wasn't the only boxer who hated Don King, who cancelled his trip to Melbourne when Mike Tyson was convicted of rape, and instead sent his stepson Carl King. Azumah promptly banned Carl from his hotel after making a call to Don King in America which started, "This is your slave, Azumah." While my only pay deduction is Johnny Lewis's cut, Nelson has to pay the Kings thirty-three per cent of his earnings, with a further fifteen per cent going to his trainer Buffalo Martinez, the man who pocketed his mouthguard in Las Vegas. Azumah announced he was going to sue King and that his former manager Dr Oko and his colleagues from Ringcraft Promotions in Ghana who sold his contract to King also were out.

    Daniel Somrack, an American film-maker, was so confident I'd win the fight that he invited me to fly to Hollywood as quickly as possible to make a documentary with Thomas Hearns, Sugar Ray Leonard and Roberto Duran, the three men who already had three world championships in their portfolio.

    Claiming he was only 65 per cent fit in Las Vegas because of malaria and an elbow problem, Nelson boasted he would take me out in seven rounds. It must be Azumah's nervous system playing up, and I can almost see the butterflies coming out of his mouth. He knows in his heart he can't knock me out. Nobody can knock me out.

    We heard that when Azumah was in Spain, Don King phoned up and said, "You are putting your head in the lion's jaws. If it'd close, you haven't a hope of getting the decision. You'll have to knock him out." Maybe that's why Azumah was playing mind games. Unless he gets into the ring with an anti-tank gun or somebody gives me a massive dose of sodium pentathol, he won't stop me.

    Eating two meals a day, I was under the limit of 59kg a couple of weeks before the fight, something I'd never done before. After my early morning run, I'd breakfast on muesli, plenty of fruit, two slices of toast and juice. For dinner I'd follow an entree of ravioli with fish or steak and salad.

For months they had been tipping Fenech-Nelson II would break the Australian record crowd of 32,500 that saw Jimmy Carruthers defy nasty eye gashes to comfortably outpoint American Pappy Gault at the Sydney Sports Ground in 1953. Jimmy told me that when it was over, he went to a doctor for tests because he had been empty of energy after the first round. They discovered he had fought fifteen rounds with a thirty-foot tapeworm inside him. They called it Charlie the Python.

We got word that Azumah was training brilliantly and had bulked up in the upper body since our first fight, and the fact that he had brought a personal physician from Spain led to some suggestions that he might have been getting some chemical help. I wasn't worried about that. I was more concerned with getting myself physically and mentally prepared.

As I told you at the start I was taking those damn Prednisone tablets that were five times stronger than they should have been. We just seemed to lose track of what he was giving me. At first I was on antibiotics for my asthma and he'd put me on a breathing machine each day before I went to the gym. I had my ear drained the day before the fight and put in drops before I went to Princes Park the next day.

When I had the needles for my hands, the doctor was so nervous that he stuck one right through my hand. I was holding my left hand with my right and the needle

Peter Mitrevski and me dwarfed by basketball star Scott Fisher.

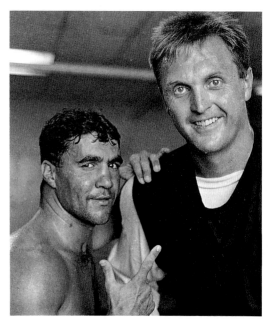

With Neil Brooks, who won Olympic gold in Moscow in 1980.

With my pal Steve Mortimer after he'd led New South Wales to State of Origin victory over Queensland.

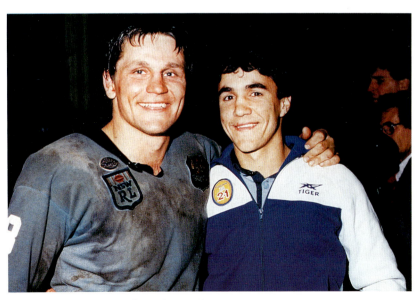

Wayne Pearce looks pleased to see me.

Australia Live: Bicentenary celebrations, 1988.

With Max Markson and some of his other clients, Duncan Armstrong, Ita Buttrose, Jane Flemming, Greg Matthews and Michael O'Connor.

Ted Whitten, Victoria's Mr Football, doesn't scare Johnny and me!

At Dom's Restaurant. Wearing the big V with some of Victoria's footy players on my 29th birthday.

With the great Sugar Ray Leonard looking on, I collect my trophy for being runner-up in the WBC's Boxer of the Year award in Las Vegas.

At the Caltex Awards with Florence Griffiths-Joyner, the beauty queen of athletics, and her husband Al Joyner.

With Mike Tyson.

Don King and Donald Trump hang on my every word.

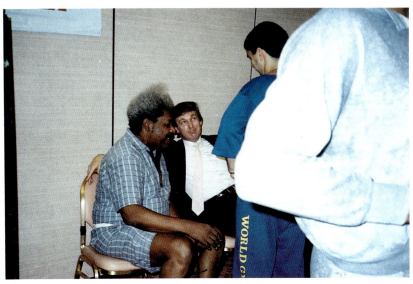

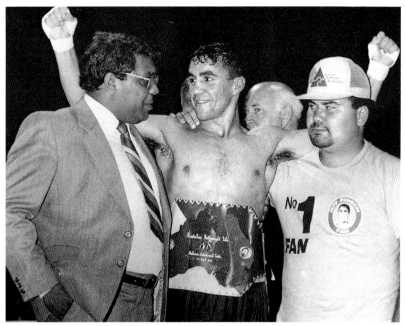

With Lionel Rose and Con after beating Tony Miller.

I visit Johnny Famechon at the rehabilitation hospital.

went right through the entire knuckle, tissue and everything and pricked my right hand. The mixture of Marcane, Prednisone, antibiotics and whatever else I'd taken, plus the spell on the nebuliser machine to fill me up with oxygen put me into Disneyland. From the time I left the dressing room, everything was a blur. As we made the long walk through the rain-soaked 38,000 crowd, my hands kept falling off Johnny's shoulders, I was light-headed and in a daze. I didn't know where I was.

They tell me when I got into the ring I forgot to bless myself. Usually I'm in a cocoon of concentration, but this time I saw the faces in the crowd. Kerry Packer, Dawn Fraser, Johnny Farnham, Paul Hogan and Johnny Famechon in a wheelchair. Little could they have imagined that the real Jeff Fenech wasn't in the ring that afternoon. Out of respect for my friend Darren Millane, the Collingwood football hero who had died tragically in a car crash, I wore his retired number 42 jumper into the ring. Azumah and I didn't eyeball each other. It doesn't mean you're macho if you stare somebody in the eye. There are a lot of good starers who have been knocked out.

Midway through the first round, my hands dropped a little and instead of moving my head as he was throwing a punch, I was standing stationary, a sitting duck. Wham. A beautiful straight right thunderbolt hit me flush on the chin and down I went. When Mario Martinez knocked me down, I jumped straight up with eyes blazing but this time I was jelly at the knees. Let me tell you that the Martinez left hook was a much better punch than Nelson's right, but this time I definitely wasn't with it. Next he rocked me with a couple of blows towards the back of the neck. I couldn't believe it. I must be in shock. I couldn't come to grips with what was happening.

In the second round I was on the canvas again from what they said was a slip, but it counted as a knockdown because Mercante applied a count. What was happening? I was still in gaga land, getting caught with punches that wouldn't normally have got through. Incredibly, I battled my way back and even won a couple of rounds. It's amazing what the human spirit can achieve. Azumah kept saying, "Let's go, baby," and I got back into the fight simply by pushing my body to the limit.

In the corner Johnny was pleading, "Keep tidy, Jeff. Keep your hands up." Azumah punished me in the sixth, but when I took the points of the seventh, Johnny said if I could keep doing what I was doing for another round or two, I could win the fight.

But I just wasn't with it and Azumah's punches were hurting. My resistance was getting low. In the eighth, Azumah saw the whole right side of my face was exposed and over whipped a zinging left hook, packed with dynamite. Wham. Nelson is a black blur as he begins to throw the bombs. Two left hooks, a right, a left and another right. The crowd is spinning and I'm on the canvas. I jump up at two to take an eight count in a daze and when Azumah storms in to finish me, Arthur Mercante stops the fight just as the towel came fluttering in from my corner. After 28 fights, I was a loser.

At ringside Dr Ferdie Pacheco, once Muhammad Ali's physician and now America's top TV colour man, was saying: "Like the guys at Gallipoli, Jeff came up the cliffs with all the guts in the world, but he came face to face with barbed wire, land mines and Azumah Nelson with a machine gun."

Peter Mitrevski was sobbing in the corner and mum and Tania were shedding tears at the bottom of the steps. It was a sad way to go out, but I'd always said if I was to lose a fight, they'd have to carry me out. I could never live with myself if I walked out of the ring a loser without giving it my all. I'd been beaten, knocked out. You can't be beaten more convincingly than Azumah beat me. I got a couple of brownie points for being humble in defeat at the press conference, offering no excuses and saying I was beaten by a great, great champion and I hoped the defeat would make me a better person. Azumah was a gracious winner, telling me not to give up on my dream of winning five world titles.

From the moment the fight was over I was soul searching. We had a big party lined up at the Metro hotel, so I went there, made a speech and was applauded. Then back to the Bryson where I walked up and down the corridor for hours, trying to work out what had gone wrong. Still searching for answers, I put on my hat and went out into the Melbourne night to pace the streets on my own in the early hours of the morning. God, if that's the best I can do, I don't want to fight any more. I was so ashamed. Something happened to me that I never thought would happen and I had to find the answer.

The next morning the Telegraph Mirror's editorial said: "Jeff Fenech's defeat in Melbourne will bring mixed reactions from the Australian public. As always with

Fenech, some will laugh, some will cry. And while, undeniably, he has not led an unblemished life, he has been a shining example of what courage and determination can achieve. Fenech's prowess in his sport was such that some of this country's rich and famous sat, hot and sticky and wet, in hastily purchased plastic raincoats in $500 seats to see him fight. So, too, did 35,000 other fans. Fenech can be proud of what he has achieved in his sport. And Azumah Nelson has proved himself not only a great champion but a gracious one."

For days and weeks Johnny and I kept searching for answers, and when I saw the neurologist, all the pieces of the jigsaw fell into place. The doctor with the wrong dosage of tablets and the oxygen machine. The women I'd had. Too much publicity stuff and having my head in the promotion too much. Azumah's preparation had been perfect, while I didn't dot the 'i's and cross the 't's as I should have. It's history now and can't be changed, but I was happy I'd found the answers.

Boxing is a funny sport. Some people love it and others despise it, but I think deep down everybody likes to watch a good brawl. It's the ultimate test. It was big at the Colosseum in Rome and it's big now. If you are good at anything, people respect you and usually like you, but if you are an Australian and become too good, the old tall poppy syndrome rears its head. The most support I've ever had occurred after the draw in Las Vegas and the loss to Nelson.

Now I'd sorted out what had happened, I became a lot happier and decided I'd try for another crack at Azumah Nelson's WBC world crown. I could take an easier path and shoot for an IBF, WBA or WBO championship, but for world title number four to have real credibility, I had to win from Azumah. I've never taken the easy way out. The three world title belts I have hanging in my house are real belts with real credibility. In defeat, I still can look at myself in the mirror and say I've got credibility because the man who beat me was by far the best of the champions in my division.

When interviewed by World Boxing some time after Fenech-Nelson II, Azumah said: "Jeff Fenech is a warrior-like guy I'd rate up there with Salvador Sanchez and Pernell Whitaker, even though he fights a different style. No matter how much you hit him, he kept coming back. That is truly the mark of a champion."

Some of my supporters took the Nelson loss as hard as I did. There is a guy in Melbourne called John, who went on a hunger strike after the draw in Las Vegas. All he has ever wanted in life is for Jeff Fenech to win six world titles. He was crazy about me. I've been to his home and had lunch with his mother and father. When I lost to Azumah, John rang up to say he'd ripped all my photos off the wall and now hates me. When he woke up that he had to live with the fact that I wasn't going to win six titles, he rang up and apologised and asked for some new photos.

Next thing I broke my sternum and I was just hanging on and hanging on. Maybe I didn't have the resistance any more. Perhaps that little bit extra that had made Jeff Fenech a champion in the '80s had gone. Maybe I had lost my hunger. The champion is always the last to know that he hasn't got it any more. You look at a video and ask yourself, "Why can't I do it any more?" It's harder to accept you're a bit older. It's like a new car. After ten years it gets old and doesn't run the way you'd like it to, so it's time to trade it in. We can't trade in parts of our body, so I just had to do the best I could with what I had.

Chapter Eleven

Mates and Ex-mates

I'VE been burnt by a number of my so-called supporters. I like to help people and I'm too trusting. Without doubt, that's my problem. When you're a big winner, people leech on to you and I blew a lot of money picking up hotel bills and tabs here and there for my fair weather friends. Maybe for a while I was invincible, but my losses to Azumah Nelson and Calvin Grove certainly have shown who my true friends are. I'm now a much smarter and better person. If you have to get burnt to learn lessons, then I'm glad I got burnt.

There is one guy in particular I don't speak to any more. I set him up in businesses, helped him change football clubs, took him to Las Vegas and introduced him to Bob Carroll, my friend in a wheelchair who set up a Jeff Fenech Trust to help young amateur boxers. Bob paid this guy a lot of money to look for and set up a business and when the shop went down the gurgler, Bob lost his money and my ex-friend walked away. Next thing Bob died. I thought so much of him that I put the dressing gown I wore when I won my third world title on the coffin to be burned. My ex-friend didn't even turn up at the funeral.

Reebok, too. I gave the company more publicity than the rest of the people they sponsor put together. I'd walk down the street and they'd say, "Look, he's in a tracksuit again." I'd refuse to go on telly unless I was wearing their gear, but as soon as I had my problems with the greengrocer, Reebok dumped me.

Thankfully people like Johnny Lewis, Bill Mordey, Peter Mitrevski, Con Spyropoulos and Mario Fenech have always been stickers, people who are there rain, hail or shine. Now let me tell you about my real friends.

Johnny Lewis would be the first to say that Jeff Fenech could have trained with anybody and won a world title, but I could never have achieved what I did or stuck at the sport as long as I did without him. With Johnny calling the shots, you could fill the Warragamba dam with the sweat that's come off my body. Johnny's special quality is that he can bring the best out of a person.

Mike Tyson calls him Mr Lewis, a rare courtesy. After I introduced them in Atlantic City, Johnny said we both reminded him of caged lions waiting to break out. It's all been said about Johnny Lewis, my father confessor, teacher, protector and best friend. I really do love the bloke and I'd kill for him. Ask the drunk who came after us with a broken bottle in Dubbo or the guy who speared Johnny into a concrete path as we were leaving a State of Origin rugby league match at Lang Park in Brisbane. Jeff Harding and I used him as a cross between a heavy punching bag and a life-sized football until Johnny recovered enough to drag us away.

My real father was so gravely ill with heart trouble

for most of his life that I really couldn't burden him with any of my problems. Johnny has always been there. The day I met him at the Newtown Police Boys gym was the greatest day of my life. He means so much more to me than just being my trainer. That's why I always had my head resting on his back when I went down to the ring for a big fight. It was him and me against the enemy and I always gave him a little kiss on the back, just to reassure him.

Johnny genuinely cares for his fighters, and often has said that to him, Jeff Fenech was no more important that a 14-year-old kid preparing for his first amateur bout. I knew that even if I was a mile ahead on points in the last round and was in danger of getting badly hurt, he'd throw in the towel without hesitation. Some trainers just sit there and watch their man getting slaughtered. Look at the way they let Muhammad Ali get punched around. Cruel, getting him to play little games like the rope-a-dope with George Foreman, who'd punch holes in a brick wall.

Take Johnny Lewis away from Erskineville, where he has lived all his life, and he'll become homesick in half a day. Humility is his middle name. Forget the bright lights, Johnny's idea of a big night out is a plate of spaghetti at a restaurant in Newtown and a few beers with his close mates. He's a prankster, too. A fun person, but whenever I showed signs of being a lair, he'd jump on me like a ton of bricks. After I won the world title from Satoshi Shingaki, I went off the rails a bit. Blokes would pick fights with me to prove how tough they were, and I'd know as soon as I hit them it would be all over the front pages. Next thing I'd be in strife with John again. He sat me down and said, "Jeff, see that door. You walked through it three years ago. Mate, walk back out of it." Of course, it was like a lovers' tiff. We got back together with bonds between us even stronger. We worked things out. We always have.

As a friend, you'd never get one better or as loyal as Peter Mitrevski. My dad loved Peter, who lived down the street and across the park from us at St Peters. Peter was his special boy. I used to mix with his younger brother Bob, but Peter's family thought I was a bad influence and would get him into trouble. When I called for Bob, either Peter or Peter's sister would come and say, "Bob's not home." He'd be there alright, with someone holding his head up against the wall by his ear. As we grew older, Peter and Bob became very good boxers, both being state champions. When I started to box, Peter's friends used to bait me every day: "Hey, Fenech. Wait 'til Mitrevski gets you. He'll punch your head in." Let me tell you, at that time, he could have.

Peter and I represented Australia at the World Cup in Rome in 1983, but sadly I was the only one to win a trip to the Los Angeles Olympics. We had some very tough spars in the gym, with some people claiming they shortened Peter's career. You see, it took a long time for it to sink into Peter's head that I was capable of beating him. I'd get out and box slowly and Peter would try to kill me. You can tell when a punch misses if the guy you're sparring with is out to get you. Peter was the kind of bloke you had to whack back, otherwise he'd kill you.

Of course, there is the famous story that after I'd

undergone surgery on my hand by Dr Bruce Shepherd, I tested it by punching Peter through the front window of my house. He is supposed to have unloaded with a big right hand while we were mucking about sparring, I ducked and put him through the glass by reflex action. You always get these conflicting stories. Actually, Peter was famous for his clumsy footwork, and when he missed with a slap, I pushed his chest, he lost balance and went straight through the window. There he was, sitting in the broken window with glass stuck in his head and blood pouring out of him. We both burst out laughing before we rushed Peter to hospital to get him stitched up.

Peter won Australian championships in three divisions, putting him up there with Dave Sands, Tony Mundine and a few others, and whatever he lacked in boxing skills, he made up for with a heart in the Phar Lap category. I wanted to pay Elly Pical's purse if he would come from Indonesia to give Peter the chance of achieving a dream by fighting for the world flyweight title. When Peter got beaten by Manny Melchor, he retired and the deal fell through. I take Peter everywhere, but it's a small price to pay for someone who's so loyal.

Life has changed now for my friend Con Spyropoulos. If he wanted it, I'd still be at his front door at six o'clock each morning to pick him up and look after him, but Con is an individual now and doesn't want to feel he depends on me. He is on a pension, and each day he gets on the bus and travels around. Con doesn't drink, but he goes to the pubs and clubs and talks to people. He'll talk about my career or Mario Fenech. If you ask Con what he is, he'll tell you that he's a celebrity and to me, he is. More than myself. Con is living life to the fullest and I'm very happy about that.

Brain damaged at birth, Con used to chase Bronko D'Jura and I when we were kids just because he wanted to be friends. Although Con is handicapped, there was a brain deep down there waiting to be kick-started. At first he went to a normal school, but he fell so far behind that they put him into a school with retarded kids. Con still didn't get the special training he needed, and all of a sudden he's in a black hole.

Con just needed someone to talk to and give him something to look forward to. At first he couldn't answer a telephone, but although he can't write, he now can say hello and take a message. I had to wipe Con's backside, clean him and feed him, which all helped prepare me for my own little boy. He came everywhere with us, and probably helped de-brutalise Jeff Fenech. If I had a retarded Greek kid as one of my best mates, people thought I mightn't be so bad after all. We had a lot of fun with Con, too. We had a special poster printed in which Con fights Humphrey B Bear in the main event. I taught Con hundreds of phrases, some good, some not so good. I'd tap his bald spot and ask, "What's up there?" Con would reply, "Sawdust? Light's on, but nobody's home to keep the burglars away."

The night I won my first world title, 26 April, 1985, was Con's twenty-second birthday and what a celebration. There was a champagne shower and a birthday cake as we stood on the bar of the Marrickville Hotel, with me wearing the red and gold world title belt. Helping Con come from nothing to enjoy life so much has made me appreciate the world a lot more.

It's funny, but Tania Foster and I now are better friends than when we were going out together and there are no hassles about me seeing Beau whenever I want to. Tania is a house-mum because Beau is a full-time job. She takes him to school, picks him up and takes him to tennis lessons. Tania is happy and I'm happy and we're both happy for each other. I wouldn't care if my son had the potential to be the best boxer in the world, I wouldn't let him box. Anyway, he prefers tennis and golf.

Kerry Packer is the smartest man in the country as well as the wealthiest and he and his son James are very good friends of mine. After he had his near fatal heart attack playing polo, I did Mr Packer's training program when he was working his way back to health. He's big, he's strong and the way he bounced back after that makes you wonder if he'll ever die. When Azumah Nelson beat me in Melbourne, Mr Packer and James came up to my hotel room for a chat and he was with me the night I retired after fighting Marcos Villasana. I hate putting my hands in ice, but that night at Silvers nightclub he got an ice bucket and made me put my busted hands in it to relieve the swelling.

Mr Packer has always shown me the utmost respect and has treated my friends the same way. Once he took a group of us on a private plane to have some fun in Las Vegas. There were polo players, some of my mates and lots and lots of people. We stayed at Caesar's Palace and it was the trip of a lifetime. I met James Packer with John Singleton one night. We went out to dinner, our friendship flourished and at one stage James wanted to become my manager. James doesn't take any short cuts and is determined to do it the hard way, just like his dad. He can mix with anybody and when he and his father talk, you sit and listen. When you talk about people with unbelievable desires, nobody can top Kerry Packer. If he wants something, he'll just go out and get it. He should be Prime Minister.

Theo Onisforou, whom I met through James Packer, definitely helped me double my ring earnings when he took over as my manager. Theo was my barrister when I was summonsed to appear before the New South Wales Boxing Authority after the little scuffle at Mt Pritchard Community when I once again was the victim of being Jeff Fenech. He is a very smart operator and now my boxing career is over, I always talk to Theo if I have a problem.

Theo has been criticised for playing hardball with Bill Mordey, to whom I owe everything, but he plays hardball with everybody. When Don King tried to tie me up, Theo beat him at the negotiating table. Some people take jobs knowing they are going to be disliked, and Theo didn't mind at all doing that for me. That's what I hired him for and invariably he got me a better deal. When I fought Azumah Nelson in Melbourne, I as the challenger got double what the champion was paid, yet Theo has never taken a cent from me.

Nobody had to introduce Mike Tyson and me. We were at the World Boxing Council award night in Las Vegas shortly before Mike knocked out Frank Bruno in five rounds to retain his world heavyweight title. He came over, grabbed me and said, "How are you doing? You sure look like you can fight." Tyson wasn't very tall, but with his powerful neck and chest, he's awesome. A pocket battleship. He might have a soft, wispy little voice, but if I was stuck in a battlefield, I'd rather have Mike Tyson beside me than anyone else. Boxing video nut Mike said he'd watched tapes of all my fights, and then we sat down at a table and talked. Just the greatest fighter in the world and me. I'd had some big moments in my boxing career, but this was the buzz of a lifetime.

I felt like the little kid let loose in the candy store. Apart from Tyson, Sugar Ray Leonard, Julio Cesar Chavez, Azumah Nelson and I were presented with awards, with Tyson and Leonard named as WBC Fighters of the Year. I was runner-up, a great honour for a kid from the back streets of Sydney. That wasn't the end of it. Tyson invited me into his dressing room before the fight, and when I got there, his promoter Don King kept shouting at him, "Hey, Mike, here's our man. Fenech's our champ. He's ours."

I believe Tyson was very unlucky to be sent to gaol. I don't say he didn't do it, but I don't think he did it the way it was spelt out. There are a million guys out there who are guilty of the same offence. It happens every day and nothing happens to them, but because he was Mike Tyson, he was dealt with more severely. I mean, what was she doing going to his hotel room at two in the morning? If Mike could have met a Johnny Lewis after his first trainer Cus D'Amato died, he still would have been the undefeated heavyweight champion of the world. I don't care what people say about him, he'll always be my friend. Mike baby-sat my little boy and was lovely to my handicapped friend Con when we were in Las Vegas. He was charming to everybody. If he returns to the ring on his release, I'm sure he will knock out Riddick Bowe and Lennox Lewis.

I'm obsessed with rugby league, I love it. Boxing is a one-on-one thing and league is a team sport, but both call for an extraordinary amount of physical and mental toughness. If I could press a magic button and turn myself into one particular player, it would be Tommy Raudonikis, gutsy half-back for Australia, Western Suburbs and then Newtown. He epitomised what winning was all about. Once Tommy was bleeding in the Newtown dressing room at half-time and they wanted to stitch him up, but he yelled out, "No, we'll all bleed together." With that, he put his hand over the gash in his head and rubbed the blood all over his face. That was Tommy all over. He went to Adidas and got me the first tracksuit I didn't have to pinch and now Adidas are the people who clothe me.

Forget the talk that the name Fenech means rabbit in Maltese. In my book it stands for loyalty as Mario Fenech, of New South Wales, South Sydney and now North Sydney, and I are very loyal people. Mario is one of those unlucky guys who was always good enough but never played for Australia. As good a footballer as Mario is, I think he's a much better person. We are the closest of friends, and his football comes second as far as I'm concerned because he's just a great guy.

We call each other Canhead. One day at Parramatta Stadium, hot-tempered Mario was sin-binned and came up the tunnel in tears. Absolutely distraught, he said to me, "Why me? Why do they always pick on me?" A TV cameraman was shoving a camera in his face, and Mario called: "Canhead, get him away." With my hand in plaster, I shoved the guy away. Yes, you've guessed right. The front-page story in Rugby League Week was "Fenech Attacks Cameraman." And they weren't talking about Mario.

As a Parramatta supporter and ex-Eel myself, my other favourite players are Ray Price and Peter Sterling. Like Tommy Raudonikis, Pricey would do anything to win. Through my boxing, I was able to do lots of work and spar with Steve Mortimer, another all-time great and champion bloke who played half-back for Australia and the Canterbury Bulldogs. He always did it tough against Tommy Raudonikis, who had some magic spell he used to cast over Turvey. Dan Stains, of Queensland and the Cronulla Sharks, mightn't have won as much fame as the other guys, but when he was living with me he used to motivate me with his positiveness.

As a kid growing up, I watched all of Sylvester Stallone's movies. I have each one on video and I've watched them over and over. I framed posters of Stallone and hung them on my wall. When I jogged through the back streets of Marrickville, I'd hood my face the way Rocky Balboa did.

I got a real buzz from meeting Sylvester Stallone when he was out here promoting one of his Rocky movies. He said he was a great Carlos Zarate fan, so I gave him the shorts I wore the night I demolished his hero. Stallone said he'd send me a pair of the red, white and blue shorts he wore in the Rocky movies. Some other stuff arrived, but not the shorts. That's funny because he said he sent them.

One day I walked into a shoe shop in Melbourne, and there was Viv Richards, the West Indies cricket captain. Like all the Windies guys, Viv loves boxing and we recognised each other immediately. We chatted, and later on I went to the Sydney Cricket Ground to visit him. Viv asked for my autograph and gave me his World Series shirt, which I still have.

Apart from Viv's shirt, I've got Allan Border's yellow Australian shirt in my collection of more than 100 different sporting jumpers and shirts. I've got Mal Meninga's Australian rugby league jumper, while Peter Sterling, Steve Mortimer and Pat Jarvis have given me their New South Wales State of Origin jumpers. Alfie Langer, Dale Shearer, Bobby Lindner and Dan Stains gave me their Queensland State of Origin jumpers and I've got Henderson Gill's Wigan jersey. I'm going to get them framed and put them on the wall in a billiard room I'll build at home. I've given away most of my boxing gear, but I've still got my Olympic blazer, singlet and boxing trunks.

I've also got the black-and-white striped number 42 Collingwood jumper worn by Darren Millane, who wiped himself out in a car crash a couple of months before Fenech-Nelson II. In fact, I wore it into the ring that day, as I said. When we first went to Melbourne, I used to train at Collingwood, so the club and I adopted each other. I met Tony Shaw and Peter Daicos, great guys, but I felt the most affinity with Darren Millane, who lived life in the fast lane like a Newtown boy. Not only was he a good player, but he always had time for the kids. In death Darren was an even bigger role model than when he played because he left a deadly warning to the kids not to drink and drive. He was a big fellow with short hair, but underneath that wild exterior was a soft, lovely bloke who was a loyal friend. So much was Darren loved that thousands and thousands choked the streets of Dandenong to say goodbye. I'd like to think that God decided his time was up and used Darren for a message. Don't drink and drive.

One of the funniest guys I've struck is the comedian Norman Gunston, one of whose gimmicks is that his razor slips when he is shaving. When we did a tape at the Newtown Police Boys' Club, he started off, "I am going man to man with Mr Jeff Fenech, gland to gland combat. Float like a butterfly. Sting like a shaving cut, that's me." It was fun trying to match wits with him. Gunston asked if I took up boxing to escape abject poverty or because I liked hanging around men in singlets. Because he gets cut shaving, he doesn't like the fights.

As far as TV is concerned, I'm a sports junkie. That's all I watch. Because I'm an Allan Border nut, I stay up watching the cricket until I fall asleep. Without doubt, to do what he has done for so long and have the respect of all his peers makes him my favourite Australian sportsman.

I partied one night with Allan, in Melbourne or Adelaide, and we've been very good friends ever since. Gutsy on the field and a gentleman off it, he has time for everybody. When Australia was down, he copped a lot of flak but he never stopped giving of his best. Allan asked me to help with the fitness of Australian's World Cup cricketers in 1992, but every time I was here, they were there.

Neil Brooks, who won an Olympic gold medal in Moscow in 1980 as part of Australian swimming's Mean Machine, probably has had 100 fights in his life and won two. Both times they charged him with assault, so people think he's a mug. Actually, Brooksy is a big, funny guy who loves to go out and have a drink. One time he broke Rod Marsh's record by drinking 47 cans of beer on a flight from Australia to London but he said his dad would have doubled this. We met at the Los Angeles Olympics and became friends and when Brooksy decided to make a comeback to swimming in 1990, I helped him with a fitness program. Playing in a rock band in Perth, his weight had ballooned to 136kg, but we eventually got him down to his old fighting weight of 100kg. This got Brooksy a lot of publicity, and now he's got a great job in TV, radio, the works. He's pretty well set up, and he'll tell you first hand that I did more than anyone to help him achieve it.

There are a host of others. Reno Nicastro, a restaurateur who owns nightspots in Cairns such as the End of the World, 2000 BC and a karaoke bar. He is the one person I've met in my travels who has turned out to be a friend in the Peter Mitrevski class. Reno has come with me to Bismarck and Memphis in America, was in Kostya Tszyu's corner in Memphis. Ray Connolly, the ring announcer, is another of my favourite people. I love the man and listened to every word he said before a fight. He talks softly and politely like a parish priest and looks almost cherubic when he gets into the ring in his dinner suit. One of his early introductions was "Pre-ordained for enshrinement in legend." I liked that.

My sisters Rita and Veronica have been super supportive since day one. I've always said Rita is the best fighter in the family. If anyone picked on us, they had to deal with her, too. Rita is the sort of mum that if you were scoring a try, she'd be scoring it with you. Her son Jamie Adamo was a terrific footballer, but gave it up to become an apprentice jockey with Brian Mayfield-Smith. After my fights, somebody like Mario Fenech would be there to hoist me up in the air and carry me round the ring. After one win, I was being carried shoulder high and when I looked down it was Rita holding me up!

Veronica is the closest to me of all my brothers and sisters and always will be. I love her to death. She was the sheltered one in the family because my dad, knowing deep down what was happening in the streets of St Peters, wouldn't let her out much. Although she lives on the Central Coast, she runs all my financial affairs as secretary of the Jeff Fenech Corporation and has saved me thousands of dollars.

My eldest brother Godfrey was the quietest of the family, a bit of a loner. Eric is the noisy one, cocky and a good little footy player. He has a couple of daughters and lives close by mum. My third brother Henry and I got up to a few things together, but now he's a great dad who lives at Seven Hills. He has a couple of kids, does everything with them, and has another on the way. His wife is a devoted mother and they're very, very happy.

There are so many others. John and Lorrie McEnearney, who have travelled to every fight and been a major influence on my career. My neighbours Joan and Alan Goldie, who have been like a second mum and dad from the day I moved into the house in Fivedock. With Alan supervising, Joan mows the lawn, keeps an eye on the place and takes my dog Duran for a walk every day. Happy Joe, who built the roof on my house, came round one day for an autograph and now lives with me. He is Beau's best friend. Brian Doyle, who boxed with me and who does everything from the heart. Eddie Younan and Steve Christodoulou, my other sparring partners. Ray Giles, the trainer at Collingwood who has taught me so much about being a man. Peter Flynn, a life-long friend from the days we played footy at Simpson Park, St Peters. Geoff Mitchell and Michael Mansour, my other friends. Peter Andre, the singer.

I've learned in life that all the things that success brings contribute to failure. Some of the sucks that used to be in my entourage, guys who wanted to be my friend just because I was world champion, they've gone. And good riddance.

Chapter Twelve

BREAK-EVEN BILL

BILL Mordey is the best boxing promoter in the world, but if he has one problem it's that he is hopelessly over-generous. He wants to be Mr Nice Guy all the time, so he ends up having to fight for survival. Between Bill and I, we've made a lot of money from boxing and had some terrific times, but Bill has always poured the cash back into the sport or the punt. There isn't a bad bone in his body, except when he tells people that Dr Frankenstein, a gentle philosopher much like himself, unwittingly unleashed a monster into the world, much like he did with Jeff Fenech.

Bill once told me that if I was stripped naked and thrown out the door of his office, I'd have a suit of clothes and money in the pocket by the time I'd gone two blocks. Easy, I wouldn't even have to pick Mordey's pocket. I'd simply snip him for a loan. Bill can lose $10,000 at the races and have $20 in his pocket and he'll give it to you. Then he'd walk home. Bill has a lovely lady in Gwenda and if they had a million dollars or just a dollar, they'd be just as happy because they're great people.

When Bill came down to Dapto to watch my fifth

professional fight against Wayne Mulholland, he turned up in a limo with a driver. Obviously he had more money than I did. What I didn't know was that he only had enough cash in his pocket to buy a couple of Jack Daniels and coke. Colin Love, my first manager who had begged Bill to watch a video of one of my fights, introduced us after I'd surprised Ron Casey, Joe Bugner and all those guys who thought Mulholland would be too cagey for me. I won very easily in five rounds.

Bill was a lean, smiling knockabout sort of guy, an ex-journalist who had a cigarette in one hand, a bourbon in the other and a sharp, lived-in face that's been to a thousand parties, casinos and card games. We chatted, shook hands and that was it. The Mordey-Fenech team was born and we've operated on a handshake ever since. We've had a couple of arguments, but only when other people got into the middle and tried to drive a wedge between us.

Right now Bill has the best boxer pound-for-pound in the world in Kostya Tszyu and if he just concentrates on Kostya, he'll find his pants again. Don King, who calls him Brother Bill, offered him $500,000 for Kostya's contract after he'd had a handful of fights, but Bill said no. Actually, one of my favourite Bill Mordey stories occurred when he and I went to Memphis when Kostya had a fight there early in 1993. After my friend Reno and I had gone out, we got back to find Bill propping up the bar at 1.30am with Panama Lewis, a very well-known American boxing man who was barred for taking the stuffing out of the gloves, and Aaron Snowball, who was in Mike Tyson's corner.

By now Bill had had two bottles of Jack Daniels, no, maybe three, and he grabbed me by the arm and sat me down. Panama Lewis might have been a rogue, but I loved his company and after a while Mordey said to Lewis and Snowball, "Look at this kid's hands. You guys are expert boxing trainers. Let's see what you can do with them." Up to their rooms and down they came with scissors, tapes and bandages. Here was I at 3am in a bar in Memphis, Tennessee, having a drunken Panama Lewis bandaging one hand and a drunken Aaron Snowball the other. At 3.30 I said "Jesus, Bill, give one of them a victory. Cut these tapes off and let's go to bed." So he called Old Panama the winner, but when Bill stood up, he couldn't walk. So I took my lovely promoter up to his room, undressed him and put him into his bed like a big baby.

Whether Bill goes out of this life with money or with nothing, I'll remember him as the most generous man I've ever met. When Bill went to my fight in Las Vegas, Don King put him in row 46. Yet when Bill puts on a promotion, he rolls out the red carpet. Everybody is looked after first class. Hotel rooms, food, drink, it's always there. Bill could have saved hundreds of thousands of dollars over the years by cutting back like the other promoters, but he likes to do things with style. A lovely man.

He used to drive a canary yellow Mercedes, but while in Melbourne for Fenech-Nelson II, he slipped smoothly through the city traffic in a gleaming white Rolls Royce. Bill told me, "You know, when I bought my first old bomb for 90 quid, the accelerator pedal fell off at the first set of traffic lights." Street cunning, even in those days, he promptly sold it to a man who couldn't drive.

Bill told me that Roller would have come in handy on an earlier trip to Melbourne in his tennis writing days. Enjoying drinks in a hospitality tent at the end of the day, he noticed one of the girls in a skimpy tennis dress was shivering, so Bill took off his pants and told her to put them on. So far so good.

One of Bill's mates summoned a uniformed police friend, who laughingly impounded the pants and took them to Richmond police station. A kindly lady drove Bill to the Hilton Hotel, where the foyer was like a peak-hour rush. In strode the pantless Mordey to collect his key before turning to the gaping throng and announcing "Wonderful hotel, lousy laundry service."

Fleet Street loved him when Bill and I went to London with Joe Bugner for his fight with Frank Bruno, which incredibly had bigger gate takings than the FA Cup. The Times described Bill as a likeable rogue, which I suppose was better than Joe being called an overweight Liberace. Asked whether Joe was planning a champagne celebration, Mordey replied, "No, we'll just have a can of beer and a chop. We're too old to rage."

In spite of playing hardball with guys like Don King, who treats the boxers as little more than bits of meat, Bill remains famous for paying his boxers over the odds, explaining he has to put his head on the pillow each night, close his eyes and go to sleep.

Bill's head forever seems to hang in a cloud of cigarette smoke. Everyone knows he is a smokaholic who once cancelled a trip to Perth because he couldn't face a three-hour flight without having a puff. When in Las

Vegas for Fenech-Nelson I, Bill went to the Mirage to watch the magicians Siegfried and Roy, whose finale to their act is to make two white tigers disappear. Because smoke upsets tigers, you can't smoke during the performance, so Bill asked to be seated near the door. When the tigers appeared, he disappeared.

The nuns at the convent where he went to school had Bill pegged for the priesthood, so they took him one day to a Franciscan monastery. Although the day was freezing, the monks just had sandals on their feet. No way, said Bill.

Bill is a very, very funny guy. When I was having weight problems, Bill was asked if he'd ever shed ten per cent of his body weight. He shot back, "Most Saturdays at the track." There is one boxing writer who is in love with the Waters brothers and once claimed Troy Waters was a second Les Darcy. When this guy kept pushing for Jeff Harding to defend his world title against Guy Waters, Mordey said, "Look, if you gave Guy Waters a pneumatic drill and put him in the ring with a garden gnome, they'd bet evens on the gnome."

When Bill moved from the city to live on a country property at Singleton, his nickname changed from Break-even to Break Everything. On the first day he put on his gumboots, jumped on to a tractor and drove it over his lawnmower and through a wall of his shed!

One day when a circus came to Sydney, Bill arranged for me to get into the lion's cage and be photographed shaping up to the lion. No way. Bill said there would be a guy with a gun to kill it if the lion went berserk. I'm stupid, so I said, "OK, let's do it." Good photo. The lion played up a bit, but finally it came down the chute, stood with its paws up and I stood there wearing gloves. The picture was on the front page the next day. A week later the lion tore up one of its trainers.

Chapter Thirteen

The Greengrocer

THE greengrocer assault case finished up costing me $600,000 in contracts, as well as the legal fees for four people, which certainly weren't cheap. Oh yes, I also was fined $300 after a magistrate in Balmain Local Court found Jeff Fenech, tall poppy, guilty of assaulting George Mouyzaya.

Originally the hearing was set down for one day, but continued for eight days, stretched over seven months. I was found guilty of something I didn't do and it left me with a very bitter taste in my mouth about the people who run our law, the ones who are supposed to be looking after us. I was accused by one policeman of being a standover man for the fruit industry, some sort of mean Mafia type. Then I was charged with witness tampering, a charge which later was withdrawn by the Director of Public Prosecutions.

God, I went to that fruit shop in Leichhardt to see a retarded kid John Barisa, somebody who needs help and somebody that I've given plenty of help to. I paid him $150 a week to wash my car three times and I used to drive him home and bought him clothes, including

American military gear in which he hunted a fictional half-human half-goat character called Goat Man. I love helping handicapped people and the underprivileged. I'm sure that if you give any of them a little bit of confidence, they improve. Look at the results we've got out of a bloke like Con.

I don't deny that I argued with Mouyzaya when I went to his shop with my good friend Peter Mitrevski, my brother-in-law Mick Adamo and Max Semrani. I don't deny that Max Semrani had a fight with him. He admitted as much in court. Yet I had to spend eight days in court for such a measly little thing I didn't do.

As I told Balmain Court, if I wanted to punch Mouyzaya, I could have punched him once, walked home and he would have woken up ten minutes later. I threw hundreds of punches a day with pinpoint accuracy during training and would be able to knock out a man of Mouyzaya's size very easily. I had had three operations on my hands and would not dream of throwing a punch without gloves or padding. I had just signed for the biggest fight of my life. Would I be stupid enough to risk a $2 million payday by knowing my hands could balloon up if I used them to throw punches.

The case was bound over until March, but in the meantime I'm charged with interfering with a witness. It was a nonsense, but witness tampering isn't the nicest thing to have hanging over your head when you're fighting for a world title. Azumah knocked me out and my dream of winning four world titles was knocked for a loop. Finally, in June, 1992, magistrate Peter Miszalski handed down his verdict. Peter, Max and I were found guilty of assault and fined the piddling amount of $300. Mick was found guilty and fined $200. Convictions were awarded against us, too. I couldn't believe it. The small fine reflected the trivial nature of the event and Chris Murphy, who was most helpful, said it would not be financially viable to appeal.

Two months later, in Balmain Local Court, the same magistrate Peter Miszalski said the Director of Public Prosecutions had asked to withdraw the witness tampering charge, with the Crown agreeing to pay my costs of $600. The charge was a serious one, but I think it was proven that I didn't do what they had alleged I did. It preyed on my mind and affected my work in the boxing ring, but now it was over. I was going home to look after my little boy and train hard in the hope of getting a third crack at Azumah Nelson.

However, as a result of the court case I lost contracts worth more than $600,000. Reebok cut my sponsorship and I lost a separate $100,000 contract for a Jeff Fenech fashion label. So much for loyalty. I hope nobody in the country buys another pair of Reeboks. I wear Adidas now and I wear it for nothing. It's much, much better gear. I went out of my way to wear Reebok during the six years I was with them, getting Reebok more publicity than the rest of the people they sponsor put together, yet they didn't even wait to find out if I was innocent.

Chapter Fourteen

POSTSCRIPT

I USED to worry how history would judge me, but now I don't care. People can think whatever they want. When I wake up in the morning and have my shower and brush my teeth, the guy who stares back at me from the mirror is the only one I have to answer to. The Jeff Fenech I see now is happy with life and much, much more mature. Boxing took me off the street and made me rich and famous, but I was a victim of the tall poppy syndrome. Now boxing is out of my system, I can get my life back on track.

I'm very proud of what I achieved in my boxing career, and if I did pursue it for a little too long, well, it's just that I wanted to prove to myself that I had something that just wasn't there any more. In my last fight against Calvin Grove on 7 June, 1993, I tried my best and it just wasn't good enough. It had been tough enough waiting for a cracked sternum to heal, but I wanted to set the record straight against Azumah Nelson. Grove's big right hand in the seventh round at the Melbourne Tennis Centre woke me up from that dream. One punch and that was it. I learned the hard way that I just couldn't do the

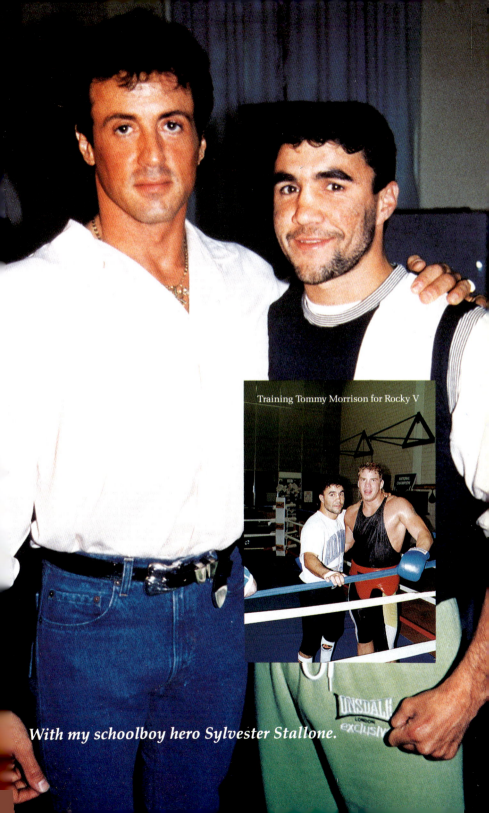

Training Tommy Morrison for Rocky V

With my schoolboy hero Sylvester Stallone.

After I'd made the weight for Fenech-Nelson II.

Beau and I in the ring at Martin Plaza in Sydney.

The day I was robbed of world title number four against Azumah Nelson in Las Vegas.

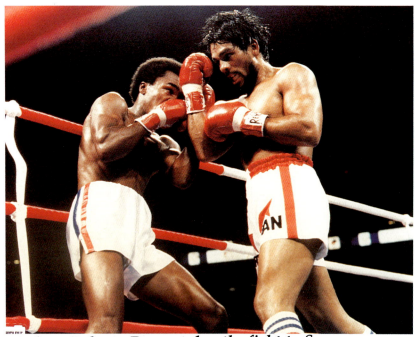

My hero Roberto Duran takes the fight to Sugar Ray Leonard.

My manager Theo Onisforou and me with a friend.

I make the weight for Fenech-Nelson II in Melbourne.

Beau toddles into a boxing ring for the first time in Adelaide.

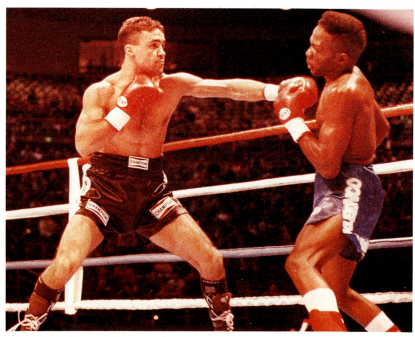

The finish: against Calvin Grove in Melbourne.

My American friends, from left, Mike Jensen, Ed Weichers and, right, Tim.

son Beau.

With my fiancee Olga

things I used to do. Reg Gasnier, the Australian rugby league captain, was known as Puff the Magic Dragon when he played for the St George club because he could conjure a try out of nothing. Suddenly the holes began to close before he could get through them, so he retired. I know how he felt.

When I was boxing, I had lots of highs, lots of controversy and I kept people on the edge of their seats. I went from one world title to two to three, the only boxer in history to do it with an unbeaten record. I could have stayed featherweight for the rest of my career and remained undefeated without doubt, but I wanted world title number four.

It was like it was never meant to be. I was to fight Juan La Porte twice for the title, but I got sick. Although he still had the big bomb, La Porte's legs were gone and he was a sitting duck for me. Not knowing I had glandular fever, for six months I trained as hard as I ever had in my life. I wasn't sharp and was gasping for breath, yet I kept pushing my body to the limit. I'd go home and say, "God, what's wrong?" The next day I'd be back in the gym trying to find it, but it just wasn't there.

Next thing I beat Azumah Nelson in Las Vegas and didn't get the decision. Two guys sitting at ringside who were supposed to be professional robbed me of something for which I'd trained all my life. That draw with Azumah changed my life, my career and my whole outlook on the sport. It knocked the guts out of me and I was **never the same boxer** after that.

I'd been on the verge of winning world **title number four**, not only for myself but for my country, and I was robbed of it. That decision left a black spot that tarnishes the sport to me. Still, I'd be crazy to be too critical of boxing because I owe it so much. I sit in my houses in Melbourne and Sydney because of boxing. I drive my car because of boxing. Maybe it's those two judges in Las Vegas I dislike so much and not the sport.

Why was I so successful as a crowd puller? Firstly, I had a great promoter in Bill Mordey. Next, I was lucky to have the charisma that captured the imagination of the public. I just tried to be as natural and as humble as I could and I fought to please all Australians. My success bred some jealousy, but I couldn't help that.

When I first started off, Bill got me to do a radio interview. At the finish he rang my manager Colin Love and said, "Jesus, what have you put me into? The guy's punch drunk. He can't speak at all." He didn't say that a couple of years later when I had a great rapport with the media. I was always accessible, quotable and I treated them right when they came to my front door. I tried to keep away from adverse publicity, but sometimes you can't, particularly when reporters are looking for a pat on the back from their boss and some brownie points. Still, I owe the media because it played a big part in letting kids and people in Australia know about Jeff Fenech.

When Johnny Lewis and I went to see the South-East Melbourne Magic play in a basketball final late in 1992 at the Melbourne Tennis Centre, we both noticed this really attractive girl. Tall, dark, stunningly beautiful. She was there with a girlfriend and as I tried every trick I knew to get her attention, the girlfriend dragged her away.

Like a detective searching for clues, I asked where

the basketball people went after a game. The Saloon. She ignored me all night and just as I gave up and walked to the door, I was introduced to Brian Goorjian, coach of the Magic. Right at this moment, Olga and her girlfriend Terese, wife of the Magic's captain Bruce Bolden walked by and somebody grabbed them and brought them into the group. I said, "I've come all this way just for you to say hello to me."

She said, "We're going to Silvers from here. Come and say hello to me there." So I went to Silvers and said hello. Her name was Olga Doukakaros and she was Greek, but born here. She worked for Chanel and also did modelling. We danced, we lunched a few times and that was it.

When Olga's parents found out she was seeing me they were dead against it because they'd read all the stories in the papers about me assaulting greengrocers. For months and months we met without anyone knowing. When I finally got to meet Olga's parents, I definitely understood what they were on about. With Olga's elder brother Peter, they're fine people and a very close family who just wanted what was best for their only daughter. When she told Peter that I'd been pitching up to her at the basketball, he was horrified. "My God, stay away from him at all costs," he said. Of course, Peter and I are now the best of mate.

My life in boxing is over, but I'm excited about starting a new life. Olga and I will be living in a lovely house I've bought in the Melbourne bayside suburb of Brighton and I'll be commuting to Sydney to see my little boy. I love Beau and with Tania and I getting on so well, hopefully I'll have no problems taking him down to Melbourne and bringing him back.

A lot of people have said that becoming successful financially took away much of the hunger that got me to the top in boxing. At first I never thought about the money, but in hindsight perhaps I did get too involved in chasing spin-offs towards the end of my career. Still, I think I was paid what I deserved because I pulled the people through the gate and gave value for money.

In spite of having a very limited education, I don't think I'm stupid. I can debate just about anything with anybody and I want to make sure life after boxing for Jeff Fenech is very, very successful. I've learned lots by being on the street and meeting people through being a world champion. I've got a buzz from reading Bryce Courtenay's books The Power of One and Tandia. So many boxers make lots of money and at the finish they end up with the backsides out of their pants. I'm determined not to be one of them.

I've been very lucky. My investments are mainly in property, with houses in Sydney and Melbourne and another place on the Central Coast. I had a couple of other houses in Surry Hills in Sydney, but I sold them. I have a Honda Prelude I keep in Melbourne and a Tarago, but the rest of the cars I sold. I was leasing the Mercedes from my company, the Jeff Fenech Corporation, but it wasn't a viable thing to do, so I sold it.

Now I've retired from boxing, no amount of money is going to get me back into the ring. Even if they offer me $1 million to fight Con Spyropolous, I wouldn't do it. When I retired after the Marcos Villasana fight, it wasn't really a retirement. I was just running away from a few problems. This time I've really retired. Not long after I lost to Calvin Grove, I was offered a $1 million package to fight another Australian boxer by a guy who seemed to have credibility and a sponsor. Whether he did or didn't, I'll never know because I told him I wasn't interested.

The biggest problem I face in retirement is that I'm hyper-active and get bored easily. I've just got to find the right thing to do. I'll keep training for the rest of my life, so maybe I'll open a health club or a restaurant with Reno Nicastro, who is proving one of my true friends. Reno has been successful with nightspots in Cairns and maybe we'll do something in the Melbourne nightclub scene. In Melbourne, there can be ten nightclubs all round the corner from each other and each one of them is full. It's no good leaving your money in the bank getting four or five per cent. You've got to go out and do something. I want to continue with the lifestyle I've been living over the last few years, and to do that I've got to look around and set myself up in business. I want to help handicapped people, too, and tell kids in schools not to take drugs, but I've got no thoughts of getting into public life. I'll leave that to the politicians with education. I don't know enough about it, so I keep out of it. Republicanism? If it's best for the country, we should do it.

I don't feel so bad about retiring as far as Bill Mordey and Johnny Lewis are concerned because they have Kostya Tszyu to keep the flag flying. I think he will go down as one of the world's greatest boxers ever. Kostya, who was a Soviet sports hero when he won the world amateur title in Sydney in 1991, has punching power that I only dreamed about. He's a programmed machine that doesn't make mistakes. Kostya wears black like Mike Tyson, jumps over the top rope into the ring and has that little pigtail. If he gets the chance of fighting the great Julio Cesar Chavez, I reckon he'll beat him. Kostya Tszyu is the best prospect I've ever seen in any sport.

You can train all you like, but if you haven't got that certain something from God, you'll never be a champion boxer. You're one step ahead, you have the reflexes. the heart, you can dig deep. I never put on a boxing glove until I was seventeen, little dreaming it all was there. Having brittle hands, I was never a big puncher but I wore people down through fitness, strength and volume punching. By the time I was in a position to knock guys out with one punch, the referee saved them. I used to build up a hate towards my opponent because he was out to take away my earning capacity and title belt. I never spoke to him before a fight and anyway, when it was over they went home the next day.

My short fuse has got me into trouble many times, but without it there is no way I could have become the fighter I was. Sometimes my temper scares me and I wonder what I might do if I was put into certain situations. Anyway, when people bait you, you can't just walk away. Growing up in a big family, I learned to stick up for myself, and if someone is good enough to give me a smack in the face or tell me to get nicked, then I'm good enough to give it back to them. I've got into trouble for sticking up for my mates, too. Same thing applies.

Sometimes it's tough being a tall poppy. "Hey, Fenech," some suburban cowboy will bait me. "You're a bloody wimp." When I was a kid, I'd never walk away. I'd rather get bashed up than walk away, but now I'm older I simply don't go into the trouble spots I used to. I can't stand the big mouths who hurl abuse at our sportsmen and women. They wouldn't have the guts to get out there themselves and have a go.

Once you've touched the sky like I did, you think you can stay up there forever, but in a tough business like boxing, it's inevitable that things creep in and pull the rug from under you. I got carried away with the women, the money and the hype and when you add this to a lot of hard fights and a lot of hard spars, it takes its toll. Only God knows where it went. We all have a limited life span in which we're only so good for so long. I had my time at the top and suddenly I faded. The Jeff Fenech that bombed out Victor Callejas certainly wasn't the Jeff Fenech that fought Azumah Nelson in Las Vegas. Johnny Lewis said that mentally I was a shot duck; that the pressure had pushed my brain box to overload. Show me a hero and I'll show you a tragedy, a famous writer once said. Well, if Johnny hadn't been there to keep telling me to keep my head, I would have come an even bigger cropper.

Without doubt, women were one of my downfalls. We all have egos, and coming from the streets as I did made it twice as hard to knock them back. It was a temptation to which I couldn't say no. You take a piece of the pie, it tastes nice and you end up wanting the whole lot. I was never a believer in saying no to sex before fights. To me, it was an escape from the pressures and a way to ensure a good night's sleep. You hear about boxers going away from their wives for a month or two before fights. God, how could they do it? I certainly couldn't. Never on the day of a fight, though. That would be outrageous and stupid.

Today as I walk up and down Florence Street, I still see people who lived there when I was a kid. Our next door neighbours, the McGavins, lovely people. Yet as I look back to my roots, there aren't too many of the guys I grew up with who have jobs. Many are in gaol and others are doing things that will put them there. Thank God I found boxing and Johnny Lewis.

I'm a great believer in fate, and perhaps failing to win four or five world boxing titles was fate's way of paying me back for some of the things I'd done in the past. I got sick when Juan La Porte was there for the taking and was robbed in Las Vegas against Azumah Nelson. Maybe I didn't finish what I set out to do. Perhaps it wasn't a fairy tale ending, but I can still get up in the morning, look in the mirror and know I didn't take any short cuts.

Appendix One

FITNESS

WHEN I get my own gymnasium up and running in Melbourne, I'll be giving personalised fitness workouts based on the Boxercise craze which is sweeping the world.

Not one of my workouts will last more than half an hour, though, because I believe in quality, not quantity. You don't have to train for an hour and a half at a time to be fit. When I was boxing, people who watched me training couldn't believe the amount I did in such a short time.

Boxercise incorporates boxing training into a fitness routine in which I'll hold the pads for the guys and girls to punch. There is nothing better than a bit of punching because it's hard work and you work up a sweat.

Apart from the padwork, people will punch bags, skip and do exercises and dumbell work. It'll take no more than thirty minutes and people will come back because it's fun, it's short and it's hard. They'll know they've done a workout.

A lot of men and women waste time when they go

to the gym. Half an hour is spent training, half an hour looking in the mirror and another half an hour showering and talking. Spending long hours in a gym is boring. I believe in short, sharp workouts in which you push the body as hard as you can in a brief time without overdoing things.

I'm a strong believer in the Bryce Courtenay theory: first from the head, then from the heart. Life is all about how you feel upstairs. Once you get your head right and set yourself a goal, everything is OK.

The people I'm hoping to interest are business folk in their thirties, forties and even fifties: men and women who don't want to spend hours slogging away in a gym. If it's short, enjoyable and personalised, they'll keep coming back.

Obviously the half hour I'll spend with fit people will be difficult stuff over three-minute rounds. By that, I mean the younger guys and girls who might be training for a specific sport. Perhaps a triathlon or biathlon. The others will work over one or two-minute rounds.

People go to the gym to lose weight, so they put them on a bicycle for 45 minutes and then get them on a treadmill to walk for 45 minutes. They don't even work up a sweat, and although it'll burn off the calories, it's very boring and not many people stick at it.

When Kerry Packer had his heart attack, I gave him a simple program, something to help him become positive. If somebody has had a problem I'll start them off on 30-second rounds and be there watching their recovery rate. It's not how fit you are, it's how quickly you recover. Do a bit of work and recover. Do it again. I'll have staff monitoring people's heart rate. I'll have a masseur there, too, because getting a rub once a week is important.

People in their fifties should try to exercise every day, even if it's just going for a little walk. If you are capable of jogging, go to a park and walk a lap. Then jog half a lap, but if you get chest pains, stop immediately. If I feel people I'm training are pushing too hard, I stop them. We all have egos, but it's pointless pushing yourself to a heart attack.

It's crucial to be able to read the individual. To know when to give them more and give them less. Johnny Lewis is blessed with this ability and I'm lucky he has passed it on to me. You don't have to have a hard slog every day. You've got to have the odd easy day, vary it and mix it up so that it's more enjoyable.

The only thing I hate more than smoking is drugs, so whenever a smoker does my workouts I will be strongly encouraging them to throw away the cigarettes. I have no problem with people who have a drink in moderation, but to me smoking is a dirty habit. People say they can't stop, but once I talk to them, hopefully I can give them the motivation and inner strength to effect a cure.

Part of my workout will be a personal motivational talk. Every time we have a class, I'll speak to each individual because when Jeff Fenech talks to people about fitness and diet, they seem to listen.

I'll talk lots about diet, inquiring about the time they eat, the amounts they eat and whether they are eating the right foods. I'm a strong believer in eating at the right time, particularly the evening meal. People sit down for dinner at 8.30pm and half an hour later they're in bed. To me, that's a no no because when you're trying to be relaxed and rested, the digestive system is working overtime.

Because of their job and travelling routine, not everyone can have dinner at 6.30pm, but 7.30 to 8pm to me is the latest you should eat. Have a little walk after dinner to relax and let the food digest a little. You should eat at least two hours before going to bed. If you can't, have a bigger lunch and smaller dinner.

Have a grain, a bran, for breakfast because it's good to be regular. If it's winter, I'll always have porridge because it gives a slow release of energy for a long time and you don't feel hungry straight away. In the summer, I have muesli. Because of my training and dieting, I'm used to eating in small quantities, so a typical breakfast for me is muesli or porridge, some fruit, a slice or two of toast and juice. No coffee or tea.

If your diet is good, you don't need vitamin pills unless there is a deficiency. If you're feeling low, you might take a pill and if you feel good the next day, you give the credit to the vitamin. I've had people tell me they were sick, so I gave them a couple of garlic tablets, saying they were special vitamins. Next thing they're feeling better, so a lot of it is psychological. I tried that Mustashi stuff for a while, but it did nothing for me. It never made me lose weight. I lost weight through sheer willpower and dieting.

After you've done a workout, it doesn't hurt to go out and have one or two beers or a glass of wine. Anything in moderation. If you feel like a nice custard tart, have it as a reward for working hard. You can always burn it off at the next workout.

I'm a strong believer in having the right intake of fluid to flush out your system, and by that I mean water. In this day and age I believe it's important we drink good water, not tap water because it's scary when you hear what's coming out of our taps. If they put a glass of water on the table in a restaurant there is no way I'll drink it.

I was a soft-drink drinker until suddenly Barry O'Keefe, who bottles natural water from the sandstone Central Coast in New South Wales under the label Down Under Springs, began to sponsor me. I started drinking the water and now it's something I believe in. I've got involved with the water company because it goes hand in hand with what I'm doing. Down Under Springs is out there and running with the big eleven-litre bottle, and the next step is getting into the night clubs, shops and supermarket shelves. It's got strong competition, very strong, but there is a huge market for it. I go to night clubs and see more and more people with a bottle of water in their hand.

When people think of natural water in this country, they come up with names like Evian and Perrier, stuff that's not Australian. To me, it doesn't taste half as good as the stuff I'm endorsing. As an Australian, I want to drink Australian water. Not only Australian water, but really good water.

Fluid intake is very important. Don't drink water between rounds, people would say. If you get caught with a decent body rip, you'll be in trouble. Nonsense. Between rounds Johnny would say, "Have a little drink." In a boxing ring you can lose up to six and seven pounds in a fight. In my fight with Jerome Coffee, I sweated off four and a half pounds and I was just a bantamweight.

Swimming is good, too, particularly for asthmatics, but it can be such a long boring procedure. To me, swimming up and down a pool for half an hour is too long. It helps you mentally to look in the mirror and see a fit looking guy. If I saw a guy with a little pot belly, I wouldn't be too proud of myself.

People must develop self-motivation and pride. If you believe in yourself, you can do extraordinary things. I've run day after day with a broken toe. I've been punched in the sternum when it was broken, and I've fought with broken hands. Maybe I'm a little crazier than anybody else, but I did it because I wanted to do it.

I would never tell people to get out there and run with a broken toe or get punched in the chest when their sternum is broken because it would be stupid. When I did it, I had to do it. The point I'm making is that your body is capable of incredible things.

Look at Merv Hughes. He looks big, but he gets the job done because he wants to do it. Merv is a winner, and who's to know whether he would have taken more Test wickets if he had been fitter. The big thing is that he doesn't shirk the issue. Still, Merv or anyone else would benefit from my fitness classes. Some of the heavyweight boxers, too.

I'm into the motivating talks, as well. There can be big dollars in this and nobody in the entire world does it better then Alan Jones. When Alan sits down one-on-one with you, he can make you feel you're the Prime Minister.

He can make you believe whatever you want to believe, but it's only short term because then it's up to you to believe in yourself. There is no one better at motivating than Alan Jones.

I don't have the vocabulary Alan has, but I'm sure I've left a lot of people very motivated and thinking. I go through my boxing career, talk about victory and defeat, how we handle these things and what makes a person successful or unsuccessful. I try to make people think.

The big thing is that I've been there and done it. People seem to sit up and listen and it sinks in. When I talk, I talk from the heart. You're wasting everybody's time if you don't believe in what you're saying. If you're false, people pick it up very quickly.

Appendix Two

CAREER ACHIEVEMENTS

Los Angeles Olympics   1984
Represented Australia in boxing
Captain of Australian boxing team

Confederation of Australian Sport
Sport Australia Award   1985
Male Athlete of the Year

Confederation of Australian Sport
Sport Australia Award   1985
Most Popular Australian Sporting Personality

Square Ring Magazine   1985
Boxer of the Year

International Boxing Federation   1985
Newcomer of the Year

Professional Boxing Association   1985
Boxer of the Year — New South Wales Region

Malta's National Day   1985
Maltese Achiever of the Year Award

Confederation of Australian Sport
Sport Australia Awards   1986
Most Popular Australian Sporting Personality

Confederation of Australian Sport
Sport Australia Awards   1986
Best Single Sporting Performance

Confederation of Australian Sport
Sport Australia Awards   1986
Male Athlete of the Year

Entrance into the Hall of Fame

Variety Club of Australia   1987
Sports Entertainer of the Year

Variety Club of Australia   1987
Sporting Personality of the Year

Caltex Sun Herald   1987
Finalist

World Boxing Council   1988
Runner-up Boxer of the Year

Oriental and Pacific Boxing Federation   1988
Boxer of the Year

Reebok Battle of the Stars Awarded to Jeff Fenech	1988
Caltex Sun Herald Finalist	1988
Caltex Sun Herald Winner	1988
World Boxing Council Winner Boxer of the Decade	1980-1989
Variety Club of Australia Sports Entertainer of the Year	1989
Caltex-Daily Telegraph Finalist	1989
Variety Club of Australia Sports Entertainer of the Year Sports Ambassador tribute	1990-1991
Caltex Telegraph Mirror Finalist	1991

Appendix Three

The Professional Fight Record

1984

October 12	Bobby Williams	Marrickville
		KO 2
October 26	Percy Israel	Marrickville
		KO 7
November 30	Junior Thompson	Marrickville
(Wins Australian super-flyweight title)		KO 4
December 15	Iliesa Manila	Fiji
		KO 2

1985

February 1	Wayne Mulholland	Dapto
(Wins New South Wales & South Pacific bantamweight titles)		KO 5
March 4	Rolly Navarro (Philippines)	Sydney
		KO 4
April 26	Satoshi Shingaki (Japan)	Sydney
(Wins IBF world bantamweight title)		KO 9

June 14	John Matienza (Philippines)	Sydney KO 4
July 26	John Farrell (England)	Brisbane KO 9
August 23	Satoshi Shingaki (Japan)	Homebush KO 3
(Retains IBF bantamweight title)		
November 4	Kenny Butts (USA)	Brisbane KO 2
December 2	Jerome Coffee (USA)	Sydney W 15
(Retains IBF bantamweight title)		

1986

April 11	Daniel Zaragoza (Mexico)	Perth W 10
July 18	Steve McCrory (USA)	Sydney KO 14
(Retains IBF bantamweight title)		

1987

April 3	Tony Miller	Melbourne W 12
(Wins Australian featherweight title)		
May 8	Samart Payakarun (Thailand)	Sydney KO 4
(Wins WBC super-bantamweight title)		
July 10	Greg Richardson (USA)	Sydney KO 4
(Retains WBC super-bantamweight title)		
October 8	Carlos Zarate (Mexico)	Sydney
(cut eye) (Retains WBC super-bantamweight title) W 4		
December 1	Osmar Avila (Argentina)	Sydney KO 1

1988

March 7	Victor Callejas (Puerto Rico)	Sydney
(Wins WBC featherweight title)		KO 10
August 12	Tyrone Downes (Trinidad)	Melbourne
(Retains WBC featherweight title)		KO 5
November 30	Georgie Navarro (USA)	Melbourne
(Retains WBC featherweight title)		KO 5

1989

April 8	Marcos Villasana (Mexico)	Melbourne
(Retains WBC featherweight title)		W 12
November 24	Mario Martinez (Mexico)	Melbourne
		W 12

1991

January 19	John Kahlbenn (Canada)	Adelaide
		KO 4
June 28	Azumah Nelson (Ghana)	Las Vegas
(WBC super-featherweight title challenge)		D 12
September 13	Miguel Francia (Argentina)	Melbourne
		W 10

1992

March 1	Azumah Nelson (Ghana)	Melbourne
(WBC super-featherweight title challenge)		L KO 8

1993
June 7   Calvin Grove (USA)   Melbourne
L KO 7

Career Total:
29 fights, 26 wins, 1 draw, 2 losses

Appendix Four

Letters
Press Clippings,
Cartoons

Dear Jeff

Right now you will be feeling like running away, thinking somehow that you have let yourself and your fans down. Nothing could be further from the truth. As a sportsman you have given your fans and your country some of the great sporting moments, some of our great highs. We have always been proud of you and we always will be. No Australian boxer ever did more for his country's pride or loved his fans more fiercely.

Yesterday, when I watched you walk from the ring feeling broken and hurt and humiliated you were beginning to experience the most important event in your life. You were going through what it takes to be a great man, not just a famous one. You were experiencing the power of one.

Fame teaches us nothing, it advances us not at all, fame keeps us in one spot, a place we try to cling to so that others will not think less of us. There is no personal growth in fame, fame is a real bastard.

But a great defeat? Now that is different! A great defeat makes us look at ourselves and learn and ultimately grow strong again. The Jeff Fenech of one defeat will be a far greater man and a far greater boxer than the boxer who fought and never lost.

My thoughts go with you, I know you are big enough to heal and grow stronger than you ever were. You are a great boxer, if you choose to continue you will still go down as the greatest two fists Australia ever produced.

Stay strong, son. I will one day write your story and what a story it will be!

Yours sincerely

Bryce Courtenay

World Boxing Council
Consejo Mundial de Boxeo

JOSÉ SULAIMÁN CHAGNÓN
PRESIDENT

July 20, 1993
O/Ref: JS-24577

MR. JEFF FENECH
Sydney, Australia.

Dear champion:

I was very pleased to read in the papers of your decision to retire from boxing after your defeat with Calvin Grove, who in your good times would have not been able to even hold your shoes, with all due respect to Calvin.

You, Jeff, had been voted as one of the best 30 champions of the world that the WBC has had in its 30-year history and you will be awarded with a recognition in the coming world convention to celebrate our 30th Anniversary in Las Vegas from December 12 to 18.

One of the dinners will be dedicated to the best 30 champions in our 30-year history and I hope that you will give us the honor of your attendance to receive the recognition of the 134 affiliated countries to your World Boxing Council.

Congratulations for your great career, for your charismatic personality that made you the most popular champion in Australia.

Best personal regards.

José Sulaiman Ch.
President

'mtfp

GENOVA 33-503 COL. JUAREZ MEXICO 06600 • PHONE (525)755-7738 • FAX (525)569-9473 • TELEX 172600CGSAME

Out of mischief to medal hopes

Nick Voukelatos (left) and Tony Pignone hoisting up Jeff Fenech yesterday. Picture: STEVE BRENNAN

By GRANTLEE KIEZA

A TINY gymnasium financed largely by chook raffles and whip-rounds is sending three gold medal hopes to the Olympic Games in Los Angeles this year.

The three first wandered into Sydney's well-worn Newtown Police Boys Club as teenagers "to keep themselves out of mischief".

Now weightlifters Nick Voukelatos and Tony Pignone and boxer Jeff Fenech have graduated to the biggest tournament of all.

Voukelatos, 20, was the first Australian gold medal winner at the 1982 Brisbane Commonwealth Games when he took the 52kg flyweight title.

Tony Pignone, 24, won a silver medal in the 75kg middleweight section in the same competition.

Jeff's seen the light and loves it

By GRANTLEE KIEZA

MAKING the grade in boxing is a lot like treading the glittering road to Hollywood.

Each year thousands of young hopefuls arrive in gyms dreaming of getting their names in lights.

Most, like the failed desperates and the unwanted of Hollywood end up used, abused and heartbroken, knowing they will never make the big time, while others perform for small club crowds there as much for the booze as the entertainment.

Some — the lucky few with a special gift — end up as stars.

Right now a boy from Marrickville is strutting his stuff in the fight game's rep theatre — amateur tournaments in places like Rome, Belfast, Jakarta and Dolls Point — and experts are unanaimous it won't be long before Jeff Fenech is an international star in his own right.

Fenech, 19, wandered in to the Newtown Police Boys Club last year and now has established himself as one of the best three amateur boxers his size in the world.

At the World Amateur Boxing Championships in Rome this week, and with only 17 fights and as many months of experience, Fenech battered the South American champion and narrowly lost in the semifinals against the champion of Asia, Yung Ho Huh.

Australian boxing team manager Arthur Tunstall says Fenech has natural talent and intense dedication.

Jeff Fenech

BOXING JUDGES DO IT AGAIN
JEFF COPS A RAW DEAL

JEFF FENECH, Australia's last Olympic boxing hope, wept with his head wrapped in a towel after another outrageous decision by the Olympic boxing jury today.

Fenech was judged the winner of his quarter-final bout in the 51kg flyweight division over Yugoslavia's Redzep Redzepovski.

But because it was a split decision, with the five judges voting 3-2 in favour of Fenech, the decision was handed over to a five-man international jury.

To the amazement of the crowd at the Olympic boxing stadium, the jury over-ruled the judges and awarded the fight to the

HOW FAR CAN J...

By JOHNNY FAMECHON
former world featherweight champion
(as told to GEOFF PREWETT)

Make the most of boxing's little Jeff Fenech over the next few months because you're not going to see too much more of him.

NO, I don't suggest he'll be the victim of a hefty left hook, more likely a victim of our geography.

Fenech, who tackles his first international professional opponent tonight at the Hordern Pavilion, has, from the brief glimpse I've had of him and from the mail on boxing's grapevine, got world title potential.

And like anyone who wants to make a bigger name for himself in sport, the arts, the theatre or movies, he will have to do his future fighting overseas.

It's a fact of boxing life.

I know that the holder of the IBF world bantamweight title wants "Rockefeller money" to defend his title in Australia.

A promoter would need at least $250,000 to stage a world title fight here and in today's boxing economic climate I doubt whether that's possible.

Fenech also has to prove he is good enough to attract a world class fighter.

But Fenech or his handlers don't want to be rushed into a world title fight.

I know we can't live in the past but sometimes we can be guided by it. I had 57 pro fights before I beat Jose Legra for the world featherweight title in London in 1969.

Fenech is far from being technically flawless.

He's a natural fighter but he is a sucker for a left hook and he'll only learn to cover up with his right hand from experience.

Like any youngster his age, he also has a dangerous tendency of trying to knock his opponent's block off once he senses the other bloke is in trouble.

I paid the penalty for doing that in the gym, fortunately not when it counted, in the ring.

Cool it Jeff.

I don't expect you to stand back and hold a committee meeting before deciding the best means of finishing off a battered rival but don't rush in throwing punches willy nilly.

That's an exit to the scrapheap.

You can be vulnerable in those positions and it sometimes only takes one punch from out of the blue to shorten you up.

The fight game is still very much in the doldrums in Australia because of a lack of personalities and today we have the dole for those down on their luck.

The dole doesn't "hurt".

Fighters like Lester Ellis and Jeff Fenech can certainly help revive boxing and there is no disputing Fenech's enthusiasm.

I was told the little bloke has sold $3,000 worth of tickets himself for tonight's fight.

He knows that if the Hordern Pavilion is well filled tonight he'll get a chance to attract a sponsor for a shot at the IBF title.

There are three world titles today and that can be confusing to the man in the street.

The WBT is the one that matters most, followed by the WBA and the IBF.

Apparently Fenech is in the hands of people who have his interests very much at heart.

They are not in a position where they need Fenech to butter their bread and rush him into a world title and that must add to his confidence.

I'll be at ringside tonight, Jeff, hoping you win. I don't want to see you drop that right hand when you rip and I don't care if it takes you 10 rounds to get the decision.

Remember, the referee's decision is final. There is no jury in professional boxing.

FENECH: WORLD TITLE FIGHT

☐ JEFF FENECH

By GREG PRICHARD

JEFF Fenech will fight Japan's Satoshi Shingaki for the International Boxing Federation world bantamweight title in Sydney on April 29, following a deal clinched late last night.

The bout will almost certainly be staged at the Hordern Pavilion, where Fenech battered Filipino Rolly Navarro into submission on Monday night to maintain his 100 per cent knockout record in six professional fights.

Shingaki will receive about $80,000 to defend his title and Fenech will get $20,000.

Promoter Bill Mordey moved quickly in discussions with the Marrickville boxer's manager, Colin Love, his trainer Johnny Lewis and IBF agent Henry O after Fenech's win over Navarro.

"The first part of the deal was clinched with Henry O before he left for Korea yesterday," Mordey said today.

"I met with Colin Love last night and he agreed to terms, confirming the contract we had signed before Jeff's latest win regarding a world title fight,"

Mordey, who said he finished only slightly ahead for his promotion of Monday's fight, which drew a crowd of 3500, estimated the world title bout would cost $250,000 to stage.

Fenech was today thrilled the world title bout had come his way.

"I feel great—I just can't wait," he said,

"I'm glad things have come through so quickly, because otherwise I might have had to wait a long while."

WORLD TITLE HUGE TV DEAL

FENECH $250,000 CONTRACT

By GEOFF PRENTER

BOXING'S little Jeff Fenech will fight for the world bantamweight title on April 29 for a guaranteed $20,000.

News of the huge deal was released today in the wake of expert opinion that Fenech is not yet ready to fight for the world title against Japan's Satoshi Shingaki.

"The fight will cost me $250,000 to stage but I am confident of clinching a major television deal within the next 48 hours," said promoter Bill Mordey.

Mordey said that Shingaki agreed to fight Fenech in Sydney for $90,000.

Fenech's manager Colin Love demanded $20,000 for Fenech, an incredible amount considering Fenech has had only six professional fights.

The big fight seems certain to be held at the Hordern Pavilion where Fenech last Monday night knocked out boyish-looking Filippino Rolly Navarro.

Ringside tickets will sell for $100 each.

Former boxing champions last Monday night were unanimous that Fenech was not ready to challenge for a world title.

"He's still learning and hasn't proved whether he can take one on the chin," said lightweight legend Vic Patrick.

"He's good, he's fast but he's not up to world title status yet," said former world featherweight champion Johnny Famechon.

Fenech will have one more fight before he tackles the Japanese.

He will be matched against another overseas fighter in three weeks time most probably at the new Homebush State Sports Centre.

His biggest purse in six professional fights is $5,000, the fee for a whirlwind four rounds last Monday night.

Mordey said today it had only been possible to clinch the world title when three major sponsors indicated they would back the fight.

John Scott, the promoter who brought England's crack jockey Lesitor Piggott to Australia, is negotiating with the sponsors.

Sponsors have been amazed at Fenech's popularity.

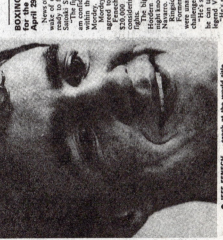

● JEFF FENECH ... crack at the world title

Fenech takes the title

EVERY minute of hard training, every drop of sweat and every bit of anger in his tiny body were fused together in 53kg of fury last night as Jeff Fenech became Sydney's first world boxing champion in 33 years.

By GRANTLEE KIEZA

Fenech captured the International Boxing Federation world bantamweight title when he stopped Japanese titleholder Satoshi Shingaki at 2min 43sec of the ninth round in a one-sided contest.

The 20-year-old power-puncher scored one of the greatest wins in Australian boxing history after battering the courageous Japanese from the opening bell.

'Street kid'

bantamweight Jimmy Caruthers, who presented the championship belt.

Fenech is the first Australian-born world boxing champion since Lionel Rose in 1968.

"I owe this title to John Lewis, my trainer," Fenech said.

"He turned me from just another street kid with a limited future into a world champion — this is a dream come true."

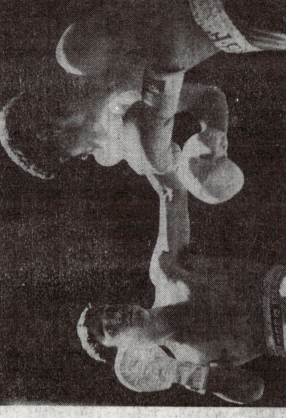

The new world champ... Jeff Fenech shows Japan's Satoshi Shingaki no mercy at the Hordern Pavilion last night — Picture: GARY GRAHAM

STREET FIGHTER TO CHAMP!

He's just too good

by RON KNOWLES

JEFF Fenech is his own worst enemy. Certainly, none of his opponents over 22 professional fights has been much of an enemy so far.

But Fenech may be knocking them over too easily for his own good.

When the triple world champion from Marrickville did his customary devastating demolition job on American challenger George "Go Go" Navarro in Melbourne last week, the question posed was inevitably the wrong one.

Instead of asking "How good is Fenech?", fight fans were asking "How good are his opponents?"

"Go Go" had been stopped-stopped in the fifth round, a battered remnant of the confident, talkative, swaggering threat that had shaped up at the start of the contest.

Fenech oozes aggression. It seems to transmit itself — just like sexuality does. When he turned up to watch his favorite footy team, Souths, in a pre-season game against Parramatta early this year, a fight broke among the two forward packs the moment Fenech took his seat in the stand.

Unfortunately for his opponents in the ring this contagion does not seem to spread to them. On the

Fenech his own worst enemy

contrary, their initial belligerence appears to be sapped by the relentless forcefield that bores in, corners and engulfs them.

Under the Fenech onslaught, "Go Go" went the same way as Thailand's former WBC superbantamweight champion Samart Payakarun, Japan's former IBF bantamweight chamion Satoshi Shingaki, American challenger Victor Callejas, Trinidad's Tyrone Downes, and most of the others who have had the temerity to get in the same ring at the same time as Fenech. They were all smashed to defeat before the fight had run its scheduled course.

Of his 22 fights as a professional Fenech has won 18 on knockouts.

Only three opponents — notably American Jerome Coffee in December 1985 — have taken him the distance. Carlos Zarate lost to Fenech on a technical decision in October 1987.

Fenech has stopped 12 opponents in five rounds or fewer. The dozen didn't have time to get dirty; they hadn't worked up a sweat before the Marrickville Mauler dispatched them.

The 12 bouts totalled only 41 rounds. In five of them, world titles were at stake.

Fenech's fans are not seeing enough of him. And that disappoints them. That is the perversity of boxing. The quicker they go, the more dubious the result.

The ease with which he wins — his dominance over his opponents who crumple under his power-punching and speed and his confidence-sapping ability to shrug off what they throw at him — suggests one of two things.

Either Fenech is the miniature Rocky Marciano his supporters make him out to be, or his opponents have been a pathetic parade of patsies — easy-beats just lining up to be knocked over.

Now that is cruelly unfair to Fenech. He has a remarkable record by any standards. He can do no better than beat all-comers, and he has done just that, usually in spectacular fashion.

It should be remembered that Fenech has not shirked any challenge.

What more can he do to convince the doubters?

Fenech's connections are hinting at a bout with Irish folk-hero Barry McGuigan. They would like the classy Celt with a clout to meet their man for a million-dollar purse in Melbourne, possibly in March.

That would give Fenech the chance to put paid to all suspicions about his ability. And if he could beat McGuigan, no-one could possibly fail to recognise him as a superb champion.

But he mustn't do it too quickly!

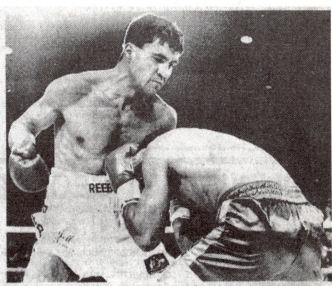

FENECH in action against Navarro ... how good is he really?

'ULTIMATE COMPLIMENT' FROM IBF CHIEF

JEFF A MODERN LEGEND!

By STEVE CRAWLEY

INTERNATIONAL Boxing Federation supervisor, Walter Stone, today paid Jeff Fenech the ultimate compliment.

Stone, speaking at last night's post title-fight party, said: "If Jeff tonight, world would have beaten the same weight in the he could become a modern-day legend. No bantamweight in the division,

● No hard feelings. A worthy champion, Jeff Fenech, embraces Jerome Coffee after 15 torrid rounds.

Story STEVE CRAWLEY
Photo PHIL LOCK

FENECH STRIKES BACK AT CRITICS

AT 2.10 this morning, how did Jeff Fenech feel?

"Very sore," explained the champ. "I'm going home to sleep it off." It had been a hard day's night.

Young Jeff, even surrounded by so many admirers at Swensons restaurant and night club in Pitt Street, looked so very alone.

All of a sudden, words counted for nothing.

The champ had run his race...and it showed.

Perhaps the turning point in last night's IBF world bantamweight fight came in the ninth round when Fenech waved an invitation for Jerome Coffee to rumble in a neutral corner.

When Coffee, who obviously wasn't born yesterday, refused, Fenech walked around his opponent and threw him into the turnbuckle.

The former Newtown junior Rugby League hooker played some of his best ever football at the Sydney Entertainment Centre last night.

He did everything bar spear-tackle Coffee into submission.

Round one was little more than a street-fight.

Rounds two and three were much the same.

Round four?

Fenech, Fenech, Fenech. Left, right to the head. Left, right to the body. Fenech, Fenech, Fenech.

Five, six, seven, eight, nine...Fenech, Fenech, Fenech.

Then in round 10, Coffee comes back. Fenech's trainer, Johnny Lewis, tells his boy to slow down if he is to hold on for the championship 13th, 14th and 15th rounds.

Fenech nods.

Coffee bobs.

"You got him, he's getting tired," screams the red corner.

But the champ is just bluffing.

Fenech, Fenech, Fenech.

13, 14, 15.

Jeff has come to prove himself.

Bob, weave, bob.

The boy can box.

He's tougher than they thought.

Fenech, Fenech, Fenech.

STALLONE FOR SYDNEY

Rambo coming to Fenech fight: P2

FENECH FOUGHT WITH A BROKEN HAND

By RICHARD SLEEMAN

AUSTRALIA'S newest world champion, Jeff Fenech, went into his title fight last week with a fractured right hand.

It wasn't until today that Fenech 'came clean' on the injury that should have prevented the International Boxing Federation championship bout from going ahead.

After providing the basis for his title triumph, the Fenech right hand ballooned to almost twice its normal size and turned an ugly purple from the pounding.

Almost a week after the bout, the hand remains misshapen and extremely painful.

"I fractured it sparring in the gym a couple of days before the fight," Fenech said.

"The doctor said we'd have to call the fight off and he sent me away to have it X-rayed.

"But I didn't go for the X-ray. I was afraid of what I might find out. I was afraid that my dream of one day fighting for a world title might be shattered.

"I'd have gone into that fight with the hand broken in half anyway. I wouldn't have cared. I'd waited too long and gone through too much to call it off over an injury."

The simple task of putting on a boxing glove was painful for Fenech on fight night.

His corner-men were surprised that Fenech winced in agony when he pushed his fractured hand into the right glove just before the fight.

The injury had been kept secret from all but his very closest supporters.

"There was no point letting the opposition know about it," Fenech said.

TOMORROW . . . Richard Sleeman explores the world of Australia's new box

FISTIC FURY

AUSTRALIA'S triple world boxing champion Jeff Fenech is hurting. The loss to Azumah Nelson last March was a blow he is still struggling to come to terms with. But as DEAN RITCHIE discovered in this exclusive interview, the Marrickville Mauler has lost none of his killer instinct or fighting spirit. In fact he's fired up like never before, itching to get another crack at his old enemy.

Artwork: ED HUXLEY

Q: Did losing to Azumah Nelson hurt you more than you originally expected?

A: It will always hurt, until I fight him again and beat the man. I beat him once and didn't get the decision. But in Melbourne there were a few things which were against me that day. I've never taken anything away from Nelson but that wasn't me in Melbourne.

Q: You mentioned after the fight something was wrong. What were you talking about?

A: After I beat him again, the people will know. I wasn't well and had been very sick leading up to the fight. I had a few problems and shouldn't have been in the ring that day. One day when I fight him again then I can talk about it. Until then I don't want to make any excuses.

Q: You've been out of the spotlight for a while now. Has the hunger which helped you win three world titles returned?

A: Yeah, I just want to fight again and win the title. I'm trying to do as much as I can training wise, but it's difficult with the sternum injury. It's really depressing at the moment just waiting for it to come right.

In my last fight, I earned virtually more than I'd ever earned before. I own some properties and I am looking at land right now. I'm always thinking about business propositions and at different ways to go about investing money. I'm quite well off. But it's all for my boy, Beau. That's the important thing.

Q: How bad did losing the Reebok sponsorship hurt you financially?

A: It has. To do what they did to me after the mileage I had given them — they should be ashamed of themselves. I have been extremely loyal to Reebok over the years. People often say I'm not a suit and tie guy but that's because most of the time I was in my Reebok tracksuit to look after them.

Q: Did they give any indication why they pulled the pin on you?

A: No real reason. Maybe it was the time. But obviously they had their reasons. I've given them more than everyone they sponsor in the world put together. That's disappointed me a lot.

Q: Has it been difficult picking up someone else as a sponsor?

A: No. Champion Sparkplugs have been loyal. They're

to do what I've done. But that just can't happen. You wish everyone could win Lotto but they can't. The hardest thing is that I've come to terms with it but other people haven't. They feel jealous and that's the

Jeff Fenech's retirement prompted TONY SHAW to pay tribute to the man and his achievements while also focussing on the qualities of a champion

Fenech is my kind of champion

TONY SHAW

IT was very sad to hear of someone who deserved the tag, "Champion" — Jeff Fenech — retire after his fight with Calvin Grove.

It was a double body blow because as an ambassador for boxing in Australia, Fenech stood supreme and it will now be up to Jeff Harding to carry the responsibility alone.

However, I believe Jeff Fenech made the right decision.

Born and bred in a working-class environment, Jeff worked hard on all facets of his trade to reach the top.

His three world titles really gave Australian boxing a kick along when it seemed to be heading for the doldrums.

Jeff was a close friend of the late Darren Millane, and every time he came to the club he was very open and approachable not only to the players but to supporters who wanted to know his future movements.

There's no doubt that Jeff will be part of Australian boxing folklore and I hope people don't just remember him for his last two fights.

Both fights were against world-class opponents and there was no shame in either of the losses.

The boxing game is a hard ask for any athlete, and it's great that Jeff has left the game with all his faculties intact.

He can now relax with his young family and get some sanity back into his life.

The man's been a credit to himself and the boxing game.

YOUR CLUB CAN HOST
AN EVENING WITH

JEFF FENECH

featuring:

- Video highlights of Jeff's fights
- Jeff live on stage delivering a special talk
- Questions and answers with audience.

Markson Sparks!
PO Box 444,
King's Cross
New South Wales 2011
Phone (02) 380 5111
Fax (02) 380 5080